Prehistory: A Very Short Introduction

VERY SHORT INTRODUCTIONS are for anyone wanting a stimulating and accessible way into a new subject. They are written by experts, and have been translated into more than 45 different languages.

The series began in 1995, and now covers a wide variety of topics in every discipline. The VSI library currently contains over 550 volumes—a Very Short Introduction to everything from Psychology and Philosophy of Science to American History and Relativity—and continues to grow in every subject area.

Very Short Introductions available now:

Available soon:

For more information visit our website

www.oup.com/vsi/

Chris Gosden

PREHISTORY

A Very Short Introduction
SECOND EDITION

OXFORD
UNIVERSITY PRESS

Great Clarendon Street, Oxford, OX2 6DP,
United Kingdom

Oxford University Press is a department of the University of Oxford.
It furthers the University's objective of excellence in research, scholarship,
and education by publishing worldwide. Oxford is a registered trade mark of
Oxford University Press in the UK and in certain other countries

First edition published 2003
This edition published 2018

Published in the United States of America by Oxford University Press
198 Madison Avenue, New York, NY 10016, United States of America

British Library Cataloguing in Publication Data
Data available

Library of Congress Control Number: 2018933293

ISBN 978-0-19-880351-5

Printed and bound by CPI Group (UK) Ltd, Croydon, CR0 4YY

Contents

Acknowledgements

I have realized in writing this book how much it owes to discussions with colleagues and friends in Oxford. I am lucky to be surrounded by people who have extremely wide-ranging interests, an ability to think beyond the orthodoxies of the day, and a commitment to new methods and ideas. Without these discussions this book would not have taken on the shape it has. Not all of them agree with me, of course, and I am responsible for any errors and overly weird interpretations. I am also very grateful to Jenny Nugee, my patient and thoughtful commissioning editor at OUP, and to Joy Mellor for skilled copy-editing. Miranda Creswell and Rory Carnegie read the whole book and improved it greatly.

As ever, I am grateful to Jane, Emily, and Jack for support and a sense of perspective.

List of illustrations

The publisher and the author apologize for any errors or omissions in the above list. If contacted they will be pleased to rectify these at the earliest opportunity.

A note on the second edition

In this second edition, I have almost completely rewritten the book; a few thousand words remain from the first edition. In the years since I wrote the first edition I have developed a more systematic set of doubts about the ways in which prehistory has been researched and written up, as well as a fuller sense of what an alternative story might look like. This book represents my first attempt to tell that story. Along the way, I have given a sense of some of the highlights of world prehistory as I see them, although, of course, this has been highly selective. Although this is a first telling of a new story, I feel considerable excitement about the picture that is emerging and hope some of this sense of excitement is transmitted to the reader.

Chapter 1
Rethinking prehistory

A profound consideration is underway of the nature of long-term human history. The major turning points we once identified—the invention of farming, the growth of cities, and technological change—were not events, but long-term processes, the effects of which were unpredictable. At the heart of the older stories was the idea of progress from small, egalitarian human groups moving in pursuit of wild resources to large, sedentary, hierarchical polities based on mass production and consumption of food and artefacts. Many popular accounts still tell a story of progress. These stories ultimately derive from the 19th century, when the inventors of prehistory assumed progress as a central trait of human history, ranging societies from the primitive to the civilized. A tale told by the so-called civilized about the rise of civilization allowed a calm presumption that history had been creating their personalities and their lifestyle all along.

A progressive prehistory is increasingly at odds with the empirical evidence of the past as we understand it. Archaeologists working on particular topics, such as agriculture or the history of cities, realize that neither represents a revolutionary change, nor were they simple and singular. Agricultural systems are often experimental, not fixed, involving many plants and animals.

Cities, past and present, are hard to define—they vary in size; some have large populations, some very small; many cities were created by societies with concrete power structures and hierarchies, but some were not; some might even have been made by those living from wild foods.

Dissatisfactions with the older model have been piecemeal, not yet combined into some broader view.

In this book, I am attempting an experimental sketch of a new approach, while at the same time giving some sense of the evidence of human ancestry and life over seven million years. Putting across human history in a small number of words, I have come to see resonances in processes around the world, which I will point out as we go along and attempt to pull together at the end. I hope readers will become part of the experiment, thinking with me as to how far it is possible to see long-term human history anew. What I can provide is a careful selection of the evidence and a framework of argument with which you can critically engage.

My starting point is that life is complex. Human beings are always enmeshed in myriad relations with the world. The trillions of bacteria in our guts, nose, mouth, and other orifices affect our health and mood, making us mobile colonies. Microbes partly depend on which plants and animals we eat, as well as the ways we cook them or consume them raw. Cooking in turn depends on heat, containers (pottery, metal, or organic), and the skills to use these and to combine various ingredients in the right sequence. All these elements depend on life beyond the kitchen in fields, woods, deserts, or savannah, the knowledge that people have, and what is culturally accepted as food. The dense ecology of our lives cycles out across the landscape and back into our houses and bodies. If we acknowledge complexity, we allow for a multiplicity of cause and effect, making it harder to see a direction to human history.

The older model emphasized increasing human control. The invention of farming, it was thought, meant that people could shape and control the environment, not merely able to take what it offered. The more secure and greater food supplies offered by agriculture meant that people could settle down, store food, develop a greater range of technologies (pottery was thought too fragile for a mobile lifestyle, for instance), which extracted more from the environment. As agriculture intensified, greater surpluses were possible and some could live without growing their own food. Specialized craftspeople, bureaucrats, and ritual specialists allowed greater planning and required the aggregation of people who clustered into new cities. Writing, calendars, and general administration led to more surpluses, storage, and trade. Much later, the urban world provided the basis for the Industrial Revolution and the world in which we now live.

This sketch, pulled together in outline before much evidence of the past had been amassed, does not now hold up to scrutiny. People often settled before they farmed; they cultivated wild plants long prior to domestication; people who lived in large settlements later dispersed to live scattered through the landscape, as we shall see from Chapter 4 onwards. Greater control is not a feature of human history and nor is the sense of direction and progress it was once thought to give human affairs. Our history is rather negotiating a mass of relationships in which other plants and animals have their own purposes which they try to impose on people. There are contingency, odd conjunctures, and events. What we lose in terms of a single narrative of progress, we gain through a greater appreciation of human variety and experiment. The sheer variety of past lives gives us hope and concrete inspiration for a future in which we will increasingly need to confront mass production and consumption, together with the damage it is doing to the ecology of the planet. Return to the past is impossible and probably undesirable, but there are elements among past relationships that we might be able to use in shaping our future.

Prehistory is controversial

For many the idea of prehistory is controversial. People whose history is not recorded in written form have been seen to lack history in two crucial ways. First, and most profoundly, it was thought that some people in the world had not ever really changed and were maintaining older ways of life in fossil form through into the present. Thus hunter-gatherer groups may have been hunting and gathering in much the same way since the Palaeolithic period, and stasis since the earlier Holocene might be witnessed among some farming groups. There is a definite politics to these views of course, with colonialists in places like the Americas, Australia, southern Africa, and New Zealand developing a notion of 'primitive' peoples, incapable of change or unwilling to do so.

Second, it might be thought that people had histories, but lacked a record of them. Without such a record, it was impossible to learn from the past, condemning people to cycles where mistakes were repeated, stymying progress. Unsurprisingly, many in the world have reacted strongly against such views, arguing that all human groups have histories and that there are many ways of recording these, through song, oral history, performance, and connection to older features in the landscape that do not involve writing.

There is also the broader question of what constitutes history. For the native historian Vine Deloria, Native Americans were more interested in place than time, being less inclined to produce a continuous historical narrative with no contradictions or gaps and more interested in the history that resides in places, which might be episodic but culturally powerful. For Aboriginal people in Australia, the whole of human and pre-human history is contained in the notion of the Dreaming. The Dreaming was a period of time, infinitely far back in the past, when ancestors moved across the landscape creating the shape of that landscape and giving it cosmological significance. A stand of trees, a rock formation, or a river were all created by snakes, sharks, goannas, or other ancestral forms and given not just a shape, but a role in people's lives, so that some places were dangerous, some had beneficial powers, and some were ambiguous.

People in the present have a duty to protect the landscape and to treat it in the right way and such duties are recorded and encoded in stories, dance, and forms of art. Initiation into such a society is through an education in these forms of knowledge, the most powerful of which is restricted to a few. Prior to the coming of whites in Australia in 1788 nothing was written down, but all significant history was recorded and transmitted in culturally appropriate forms. The concept of prehistory, telling of a forgotten time beyond the reach of written histories that needs to be discovered through archaeology, is puzzling and potentially offensive, making for difficult relationships between Aboriginal people and non-Aboriginal archaeologists. In such situations prehistory is an arena of debate over knowledge about the past that is intimately involved with control of life in the present.

I am very sympathetic to these arguments. First of all, we should never forget that power and politics always surround tellings of the past, which are not neutral or objective, but shaped by preconceptions about people, their pasts, and the possibilities of the present. Furthermore, the varied and conflicting philosophies of history can bear much more debate and comparison, with Western notions of the past increasingly thrown into relief by African epistemologies, those of east Asia or the variety of Native views around the world. As I hope to show in the pages that follow, all periods and places exhibit dynamic prehistories and histories. Our task is to appreciate, compare, and contrast those dynamisms, and to debate across cultural differences what the past means to each of us in the present.

Prehistory, in my use of the concept, allows us to understand long-term histories. We assume that real history starts with known civilizations (the Egyptians, the Mesopotamian, the ancient Chinese, the Maya, and so on), their written accounts, battles, monarchs, rises, and declines. This leaves many groups outside of the scope of history and collapses seven million years of human change into a fractional moment of time at its end. Gaining a really long-term sense of what it means to be human throws all recent lifestyles into perspective: our current, mass-consuming world is new, temporary, and fragile. It will pass away to be replaced by other arrangements.

A sense that our lifestyle is fragile and temporary will encourage us into new ways of life, rather than clinging to current forms. Assuming the way we live now is natural and the inevitable outcome of history will make us by turns complacent, fearful, and determined to shore up a way of life out of balance with the planet. When looking at the past the only thing we can be sure about is that all forms of life pass away, taking with them the hopes, fears, and desires so important to people at the time. Change will come and negotiation of change depends partly on an appreciation of the past that also provides a shape to our possible future.

Chapter 2
The history of prehistory

The idea of prehistory arose gradually between the 16th and early 19th centuries in Europe and America, but grew large and influential through debates about evolution in the middle of the 19th century. The establishment of a long prehistory is one of the great achievements of that century, as important in its own way in changing peoples' views of the world as the voyages of discovery of the previous 300 years. The discovery of the Americas was a profound shock to Europeans, leading them to question where all the peoples of the Americas had come from as none were mentioned in the Bible, and what sorts of relationships had created and spread various peoples around the world. A much greater shock was occasioned in Native peoples at these encounters.

The discovery of a long prehistory had the same impact as finding a new continent, with its own myriad and strange ways of life, except that some of the inhabitants of the continent of prehistory were definitely ancestral to those writing prehistory. For places like Britain where identity is and was an issue, ancestry was problematical—should Britons derive their ancestry from the Normans, the Anglo-Saxons, the Romans, or now the Celts—or indeed possibly pre-Celtic peoples? If Britons are people of mixed ancestry, how does one evaluate the mix of language, genes, artefacts, and landscapes that derives from the past? The same questions arise for Nigerians, Brazilians, Americans, or Chinese.

National and personal identities were problematical, and also those of race and class as we shall see, but there were deeper issues of identity that came to the surface through 19th-century debates which have never gone away. In a legendary meeting of the British Association for the Advancement of Science in the University Museum of Natural History in Oxford, Saturday, 30 June 1860, the bishop of Oxford, 'Soapy Sam' Wilberforce, confronted Thomas Huxley, 'Darwin's Bulldog', in front of an audience of some 700 people. It was a meeting of high emotion where Lady Baxter fainted, the audience gasped, laughed, and applauded, and no holds were barred (at least in the legendary accounts that are best remembered now). 'Soapy Sam' did ask Huxley whether he was descended from a monkey on his grandmother's or his grandfather's side, but the reply that it was better to be descended from a monkey than a bishop, came not from Huxley but from Hooker, another pro-Darwinite.

This half-remembered confrontation crystallized the spirit of the debate, which appeared to be about the remote past, but in fact concerned people's personal identity in the present. Darwin had long delayed the publication of *The Origin of Species*, which appeared in 1859, afraid of the controversy it would cause and the possible damage to his standing as a member of the establishment. A more complicated reception awaited his work than he anticipated, which was seized upon by different strands of thought and belief, as a perfect test of where people stood on issues of history and empiricism versus faith.

Part of the origin myth of prehistory for us is that the acceptance of a long prehistory meant a rejection of a biblical chronology which put the origin of the world at 4004 BC, and was thus part of a victory of reason over superstition, science over religion. Here lies the continuing interest of the 1860 debate which looks like a cameo version of a broader clash of social values. However, the scientists often came from a particular set of religious backgrounds, such as Quakerism, which always placed emphasis on empirical investigation and personally derived truths, in contrast to more established religious forms among which the Bible was the crucial truth.

All controversies in the 19th century were to some extent religious controversies. It was only in the 20th century and a more secular society that science confronted religion in a more simplistic fashion. Evolution and prehistory are now real shibboleths for extreme views on both sides, with the nature of children's education a crucial litmus test. Prehistorians are seen to be on the side of the apes rather than the angels, and are generally proud of that fact.

The excavation of Brixham Cave in 1858 was a crucial step towards the scientific acceptance of high human antiquity. Classical Darwinian theory, centred around the idea of descent with modification, held that the modifications from generation to generation made offspring either better suited to their contemporary environmental conditions, less suited, or made no difference at all. Those better suited had an increased chance of surviving to produce their own offspring, passing on their beneficial characteristics; those less suited were more likely to die before having offspring: hence the survival of the fittest, a biological encoding of the competitive spirit of capitalism. For Darwin, change proceeded through small modifying steps and needed long periods of time to work itself out, especially once one thought of all the changes needed to move from single-celled organisms to the full complexity of human beings.

It was impossible to see how this might be fitted into the biblical chronology of only 6,000 years since the creation of the earth. Empirical support for longer timescales poured in from geologists and biologists. For the first half of the 19th century there had been debate about what was then called the 'antiquity of man', surrounding a number of sites which might produce firm evidence that human beings had existed in the company of extinct animals, such as mammoths and woolly rhino, not mentioned in the Bible.

For Victorians, seeing was believing and the site of Brixham provided visual proof of human antiquity.

On 29 July 1858, Pengelly, a founder member of the Torquay Natural History Society and organizer of the excavations of the fissure known as the Bone Cave at Brixham, found his first flint tool from beneath 3 inches of stalagmite and in association with the bones of rhinos and hyenas. Visits were made by the gentlemen scholars of the various geological, archaeological, and anthropological societies, who were impressed by the care and precision of Pengelly's excavation and recording, but most struck by the association between undoubted human products and extinct animals coming from a different and earlier phase in the earth's history. Rapid reassessment occurred of other sites, not least those of the Somme gravels (where the later battle was fought), previously disparaged by the British as French hyperbole, where stone tools had also been found with rhino bones some metres below the surface (Figure 1).

Having visited Brixham and Abbéville in northern France, Sir Charles Lyell, Britain's most influential geologist, put aside his earlier scepticism about the 'age of man' and addressed the British Association of the Advancement of Science meeting in Aberdeen on 18 September 1859. For Lyell to change his mind was a sign that the British intellectual establishment was opening up to the possibility that prehistory was immensely long, placing recent ways of life in stark perspective. In his talk Lyell mentioned in passing the forthcoming publication of a book which, he felt, would have some influence on thinking about issues of timescale and the relationships between people and nature—this was *The Origin of Species*, to appear on 24 November 1859.

Archaeologists and anthropologists have taken two basic routes to understanding human variety and unity. The first derives from the social evolutionary approaches of the mid-19th century where our similarity as a species was stressed and effort was directed

1. The St Acheul gravel pit, Somme Valley, France. The photograph was taken on 27 April 1859, and shows a workman pointing at a hand axe in the Ice Age gravels.

towards understanding how humanity as a whole progressed through stages like hunting and gathering, farming, the development of states, and, most importantly, civilization.

Social Darwinists, so-called, ranging from Herbert Spencer to Pitt Rivers and E. B. Tylor, struck by the force of Darwin's views, were attracted by the possibility of a single theoretical basis for approaches to the humanities, which also chimed with their desire to found archaeology and ethnology as sciences. The 'onwards and upwards' view of prehistory was predicated on a belief in progress, implicit in which was the idea that not everyone progressed at the same rate or to the same degree. Only those of European descent made it through the full gamut of historical stages to become rational, civilized, democratic, and energetic, leaving less progressive others in their wake, still remnants of earlier stages of world history, in the form of Australian Aboriginal people, African peasant farmers, or the more 'static' civilizations of various parts of Asia.

It is not hard to see why progressive and unitary views of human life were unattractive to many, including some of European descent.

The 20th century

At the beginning of the 20th century, an alternative set of views was promulgated by Boas in America, but working from the intellectual framework of a German tradition which emphasized the local specificity and integrity of human cultures. Culture was later to be defined by the archaeologist Gordon Childe as a constantly recurring set of traits, such as artefacts, houses, burials, food, and so on, behind which lay similarities harder to discern archaeologically such as of kinship, language, and customs. Childe's thought combined culture's historical and evolutionary dimensions.

Cultural historical views saw the world as a mosaic of cultural forms, each with their habits of life, ways of seeing the world, and histories. Each culture could only be understood in its own terms and it was variety that was characteristic of human life, not unity. Bruce Trigger's history of archaeological thought emphasizes alternation between approaches stressing unity, such as the early evolutionary approaches of the later 19th century, which made a resurgence between the 1950s and 1970s, and those stressing difference.

Boas's culture-historical views, emphasizing different local historical trajectories, made something of a come back in the 1980s as postmodernist thought raised doubts about the scientific ambitions of an evolutionary archaeology, and made a broader critique of a possible Western objective viewpoint, stressing the need to understand other forms of life in their own terms.

Today our questions have shifted away from why some people did not ascend to the top rung of the ladder of progress and towards how people created worlds for themselves that made internal sense. Indeed, many now question whether these local worlds can be encompassed by a single scheme, especially one developed to make sense of the European past.

Also, an emphasis on technological change has been replaced (for some at least) by an enquiry into how people construct worlds for themselves through putting together varying skills and techniques, developing particular sets of social, physical, and intellectual skills in the process. Human beings have a huge range of potentials; cultural forms and histories involve developing some of these skills but neglecting others.

Australian Aboriginal people were described as the virtuosos of the human mind by the anthropologist Lévi-Strauss because of the huge amount of genealogical and cosmological knowledge they developed and maintained, putting much less emphasis on the creation and use of material things. A set of cultural forms in which knowledge is power challenges the prehistoric archaeologist whose main evidence is artefacts. But it does alert us to the idea that cultures cannot be measured along a single axis, as more or less complex, still less better or worse, but rather as being different. Cross-cultural comparison is necessary, to give a sense of human variety, not to measure everyone with the same yardstick.

Our understanding of the long history of humanity has been greatly enriched over the last few decades by the huge amount of high-quality archaeological evidence from all continents and all periods. Interestingly, this new evidence has undermined long-held pictures of humanity's past, rather than confirmed them. Inevitably, there is considerable debate and disagreement among archaeologists as older views are challenged.

The dominant older picture derives from Enlightenment thought crystallized in the 19th and 20th centuries around an idea of progress. The most persuasive proponent of the 'onwards-and-upwards' view was the Australian archaeologist, Gordon Childe. Childe thought that there were three big revolutions in human history—the Neolithic, the Urban, and the Industrial—and that both life in towns (first occurring 3500 BC) and recent industrialization were eventual outcomes of the adoption of farming, which was thus the crucial moment.

The Neolithic was revolutionary for Childe because the adoption of domesticated plants and animals provided a greater security in food supplies, allowing for control over the environment, rather than life as a hunter-gatherer at its mercy. The production of a secure food supply allowed people to settle down and a sedentary life provided the need and the leisure to produce more varied and sophisticated material culture, such as pottery, textiles, ground stone, and houses, with later experiments in metal technology.

Farmers not only altered nature through domestication of plants and animals, but according to Childe created new substances which do not occur ready-made in nature. Pottery, wool, and flax were concrete manifestations of a more rational appreciation of nature and its properties.

A further innovation of Childe's thought was to bring in a gendered aspect. He attributed many innovations in agriculture and cuisine to women, as well as pottery making, spinning, and weaving. The Neolithic revolution could not have been more profound, altering people's relationships with nature and with each other. All the innovations Childe highlighted concerned production, containing the assumption that the advantages of his various inventions were so self-evident that they would be immediately adopted.

These three revolutions were political and economic. Farming changed the basis of food production and, it was thought, food supplies became more reliable. Mass living in cities required surplus food to support those—craftspeople, bureaucrats, priests, rulers—who did not grow their own food. Farming provided the necessary basis for urban life, which saw too the start of industry, and mass production and consumption.

Millennia later this ushered in the profound political and social consequences connected to the Industrial Revolution. One revolution built on another in a progressive sequence leading to the Western industrialized nations in which most of Childe's readers lived.

An emphasis on the importance of the Neolithic revolution created two phases of prehistory. The first was very long, stretching from the origins of humanity to the birth of farming, a period encompassing some 99 per cent of human history. During this seven-million-year period people were thought to live as mobile, egalitarian hunters and gatherers, gathering wild plants and hunting wild animals. Analogies were made between contemporary hunter-gatherers, who lived mainly in deserts, rainforests, and the Arctic, and those of the Palaeolithic and Mesolithic.

Much effort was expended between the 1960s and 1980s in defining a so-called 'global hunter-gatherer model' looking at how hunter-gatherer lifestyles were influenced by climate and ecology. For instance, it was seen that groups living in highly seasonal climates in higher latitudes developed complex forms of food storage to get them through long winters. Foragers in tropical rainforests had access to food all year round and lived by direct, rather than delayed, return.

Two important assumptions lay behind the global hunter-gatherer model. First, for people living from wild foods, the environment was the crucial determinant of life, so that modelling the environment allowed a fairly direct reading of the yearly round, the nature of technology, storage, group size, and social arrangements. Second, it was further assumed that there would be universals across hunter-gatherer lifestyles in different times and places. Groups today could provide keys to those in the past, so that Arctic hunters of the recent period would allow a privileged view into hunters of the last Ice Age.

Both of these assumptions are now questioned. Even in what appears the most constraining of ecologies, such as the Arctic, there is considerable latitude in how people shape their lives. Ecology and climate are important influences, but are not in any way determinant. Furthermore, if we now take a more holistic view of life, it is much more difficult to make very detailed comparisons across space and time. Ice Age hunters lived on large mammals, such as mammoths, woolly rhinos, and reindeer, most of which are not around today, and the extinct species would have influenced the lives of those still extant (such as reindeer).

The tools, art, language, and social arrangements of Ice Age hunters all differed from the present-day Arctic groups and hence most of the crucial things that make us human. All forms of life need to be appreciated in their own terms and, although judicious comparisons can be made, direct analogy from one period and ecology to another is rarely possible.

The second phase of human life was ushered in by farming. Agriculture, it was thought, was a relatively sudden invention, allowing people to live a settled lifestyle leading to population growth and a greater range of material things, including pottery and later metallurgy. The domestication of plants and animals led to a greater organization of the landscape, which became more recognizable to modern eyes, with fields, grazing land, trackways, villages, cemeteries, and sacred sites. Nature was tamed through farming, society domesticated and set on a progressive course leading to people like ourselves. Long-term history had a comfortable inevitability to its form and direction.

Developing new views

Over recent years important elements of this scheme have been thrown into doubt, as we will see in Chapters 4 to 6. Generally we are less certain of progress than were people of the 19th and early 20th centuries. Technology can fuel rapacious urges, as well as increasing security and comfort. The effects of people on their environment are as often destructive as beneficial. More empirically, we now see more continuity between the Palaeolithic and Neolithic in the modes of cooking, the plants used, the widespread use of material culture, and the existence of settled life. Many of the features thought first to occur in the Neolithic, like pottery and housing, were the inventions of Palaeolithic hunter-gatherers, with pots diffusing later into the farmers' world.

Settled life long predates the development of farming in areas like the Levant, with people living in houses and other facilities from at least 20 kya (thousand years ago), for parts of the year at least, grinding and cooking wild grasses at sites like Ohalo II in Israel. From here there was a very slow development of different forms of household and village, with people sometimes cultivating wild grasses and hunting species like gazelle in such a controlled manner that it becomes hard to distinguish from herding. When farming did emerge, it was not one thing but many, so that the sites of the so-called Pre-Pottery Neolithic B (PPNB) period saw an explosion of experimentation around the so-called Fertile Crescent from the Jordan Valley, north through the Levant to

Syria and southeastern Turkey, and round into the rivers of Iraq and the hilly flanks of Iran.

New local landscapes were created as people moved less, known in intimate detail not just by their human inhabitants but by the animals moving across them and plants seeking beneficial growing conditions. Connecting up these newly local ways of life was the longer-distance exchange of shell beads, varieties of stone, and materials of limited occurrence like bitumen. From 8000 BC in Anatolia people started experimenting with copper, first cold working native copper and then heating it to create a greater range of shape and colour. Archaeology is developing a sophisticated range of techniques for matching the chemical or mineral composition of stone, pottery, and, later, metal, with various outcrops of origin.

Maps of the movement of chemically distinct materials can be interpreted in terms of trade and exchange. Similarly, the human body takes in water and food given chemical composition by their local geology. People who move from one distinctive local geology to another take their earlier chemical signal with them. The combination of the local and long-distance connections has been created and recreated over the last 30,000 years, gradually giving a smaller scale to the cross-species communities of which humans are part. Domestication brings dependency. Sheep rely on people for movement between pastures, protection, and care; people rely on sheep for meat initially, and later milk and wool. Mutual reliance rests on mutual understanding. Humans are unique in the range of mutual relationships they can enter into with other species, but all species develop a working understanding of others of importance to them.

Instead of a global and progressive movement over the last 10,000 years we can see the creation of many different ways of life embedded within broader networks of connection. Each way of life has its own set of directions, not necessarily moving towards

18

farming, cities, or some other outcome familiar to us. The only sense of direction is through a gradual broad accumulation of technologies and techniques. Once important things are developed, they do not seem to disappear from humanity's repertoires, although they might be given up locally.

We rely today on sheep, cows, horses, wheat, barley, and oats, all domesticated long ago. Pottery came into being at least 20 kya, and although individual areas may have become aceramic, pottery has never disappeared globally. From urban life in Mesopotamia almost 6 kya derives the fast pottery wheel, metalworking techniques like granulation and filigree, yeast, dates, and more sophisticated textile making. All of these are still with us. There was a gradual accumulation of techniques over the last ten millennia, which formed the basis for the one obvious discontinuous change: the Industrial Revolution.

One of Gordon Childe's achievements was to provide a definition for archaeological cultures, as we have seen. We still recognize differences in material culture across the world, but instead of cultures we would talk of communities of practice. Particular artefacts, houses, and landscapes were part of various structures of habit, local ways of making a living, with their own logics, ends, means, and outcomes. Crucially, however, we do not see communities of practice as being neatly divided into cultures. Rather they are more like a Venn diagram, with a series of overlapping ways of acting, some shared with neighbours and others not. For example, from southeast England in the middle Bronze Age (c.1500 BC) are found fields in a number of areas with similar layouts, but across their distribution are different forms of pottery and metalwork.

Some elements of the field systems are similar to those on the near continent, with some bronze artefact types shared between the Thames and Seine valleys. As one moves away from both these valleys bronzework changes, indicating they were important corridors of communication. Houses in England are round, those in France rectangular. There was clearly movement of people, artefacts, and ideas in the Bronze Age, but also people were creating their own local ways of life, by taking some elements from the broader cultural milieu and developing others for themselves. While we can see a complex set of similarities and differences, people living either side of the channel were by no means a single cultural group, although those who travelled would have recognized familiar aspects of life elsewhere. Where Childe's map represented a mosaic of difference, ours is more like a kaleidoscope with mixing and shifting colours.

Childe's history was economic and political. Both these terms need rethinking and I would start this through the concepts of understanding and intelligence. Human life succeeds in the degree to which we appreciate and understand the full set of relations through which we live. Again, my view would not centre on progress. Human intelligence has not improved or developed since fully modern humans arose. Rather it has shifted and changed as shaped by the world in which people lived and as they too shaped that world.

The locus of human understanding is the body. The structure and advantages of the human body are well known: our opposable thumbs, large brains, ability to walk on two legs, which frees the hands, binocular vision, and overall coordination of perception and action. But it is also the plasticity of the human body which is really impressive, which is measured by the range of things a body can be taught to do within any one culture or across cultures. In the Western world, playing the violin, making furniture by hand, performing surgery, playing football, working in a laboratory, cooking food, working on an assembly line, or gardening all involve skills some of us possess, but many do not.

Looking back we can see hand axes, complex textiles, field systems, or fine goldwork, all of which needed skills to make but also to use. Skills often involve the whole body; even those practiced in a static and sedentary manner require the correct bodily posture and attitude. Very rarely can a whole task be carried out by a single person. Weaving and dyeing woollen cloth draws on past labour in rearing the sheep, shearing them, cleaning the wool, and spinning and dyeing the yarn, which is then woven with attention to tension, pattern, and form. Clothing fashions changed in the deep past, as well as in the more recent world. The manner in which clothes are worn varies from one individual to another, and the wearers must understand cultural codes to wear the right thing at the correct time. All these actions are easy to list, but may take many years to learn and fine social judgement to execute.

My colleague, Lambros Malafouris, has come up with the idea of metaplasticity to describe the relations between people and their many worlds. Neuroscientists talk about the brain being plastic. The brain is like a muscle in that particular areas will increase in size if they are used more than others and this will depend on the pattern of activities of the owner of the brain. These activities derive from the material world which the person inhabits, as well as the routines, technologies, and techniques with which they are most engaged. In a reciprocal fashion, changes in human skills, deriving from the exigencies of life, will bring about new forms of material culture.

Archaeologists are extremely aware of the changeable nature of artefacts over time and space, as classifying differences in artefacts helps us deal with variety over time and space. Just as the brain is plastic, so too is the artefactual world. Bodies, brains, and materials are all plastic, changeable, and mutually shaping, so that Lambros's idea of metaplasticity is an important means of understanding complex connections. Body, brain, and material things are linked, but none is primary, a cause from which effects are derived. Instead people and their worlds bring each other into being, through processes of knowledgeable action and mutual understanding. All elements are changing all the time. This is a very different starting point from one in which environmental or economic change is primary. Alterations in the world around people are important, but parts of networks of change, which people also help shape.

Metaplasticity underlies world history, giving it a dynamism and lack of direction that we see as the variety of human life, past and present. My main aim in what follows is to provide some sense of the dynamic variety of life, the additions made over time to materials and techniques, which generally lack any direction, apart from maybe those we assign retrospectively.

An important foundation to people's lives in all times and places was a model of how the world works. I would argue that all models of causality are composed of three elements: magic, religion, and science (to use terms that make sense to us today). Briefly put, magic involves some element of animism, in which the world as a whole, and not just living things, is seen to animate with purposes and intentions, and this includes landscape features, rocks, trees, and rivers, as well people, plants, and animals. Things we might think of as lacking will and intention—a sword, a cloak, a mountain—must rather be approached with care, respectfully and appropriately. In contrast to magic, religion posits a god or pantheon of gods and, when institutionalized, creates places of worship within sacred landscapes.

Science (the most anachronistic of these terms) involves an appreciation of the physical properties of things, so that when building a house, timbers of sufficient strength to support the roof must be chosen; when cooking, the right ingredients are needed and must be included in the correct order, with the application of the correct degree of heat. When combined together into a consciously articulated scheme or something more implicit, magic, religion, and science compose a model of the way the world works which allows for human action, the influence of elements of the universe beyond human reach and the more technical aspects that can be understood and respected. Modes of causality shape, and are shaped by, human desire. Our wants and desires derive from what we think possible and proper to take from the world. Modes of causality are also linked to human power structures. Power arises from controlling the world and the human productive action that shapes the world.

Taking all these points together we arrive at another difference from Childe's view of culture. Human cultural forms are not just made up of humans, but involve integral and intimate links with landscapes, plants, animals, houses, cemeteries, artefacts, and so on. In the view I'm developing here, human identity does not stop at the boundaries of the body, but is made up of a composite of people and things in dynamic relations. We are what we eat, but also the animals we keep, the sorts of axes, textiles, or pots we have: to be fully human is to participate in and with the non-human. Because of the complexity of relations that make us up, humans are always in a state of becoming, not being. History does not unfold through a straightforward linear trajectory under increasing human control and it has no overall sense of improvement or progress, moving instead from one state to a different one.

In order to write our prehistories, a commitment to holism is necessary. We need to understand the full range of relations people were engaged in at any one time. These relations are always dynamic and unpredictable. Dynamism derives not just from humans, but rather from all the material relations making up people's lives. All are causative, but none is the sole cause. We are not looking for cultural or environmental determinism and indeed it is not clear where the boundary between culture and environment should lie.

All factors are refracted through the human body, which is a changing locus of skills, appreciations, and emotions. Analyses of the body, deriving from genetics, the chemistry of human bones, or of the microbiome trapped in tooth plaque, is providing us with vital new sets of information as starting points for grasping the totality of our relations. How bodies are enskilled to make and use a great variety of artefacts has long been a key area of archaeology, but now the links between the architecture of the body and the properties of materials are being understood in novel ways. In what follows, I hope to give a sense of the complexity of the relations surrounding and shaping humans, as well as immensely long timescales over which these have played out. Let us start with our deepest histories.

Chapter 3

In the beginning—African origins and global movements

We gain a sense of time and change through our own experience of life. By the time we are adults we have a good notion of the changing of the seasons, so that phrases like 'the hottest June in forty years' make some sense to us; the power of both birth and death hit home, and the ageing of the body becomes an increasing reality. Our understandings of timespans are limited by biography. To grasp the seven million years over which our ancestors evolved is both disorienting and a profound philosophical challenge. This is true too of professionals, although we are superficially used to talking in terms of millennia or millions of years.

Our earliest known ancestor lived in the warm period known as the Miocene (23.03–5.3 million years ago (mya)). The world was then very different. North and South America had not yet joined into a single continent; grasslands were expanding across the globe and grasses became various, leading to more numerous herbivores; Eurasia joined with Africa, severing a link between the Mediterranean and the Indian Oceans; mountains uplifted in North and South America, with rifting in east Africa creating a rain shadow effect initiating a contrast between a wet west Africa and a drier east; Australia continued to drift northwards. All this had effects on circulation systems in the oceans and atmosphere, and furthermore by the late Miocene the planet started to cool. Human ancestors split off from the other great apes in the late Miocene, with apes living generally in wetter, more forested conditions.

It used to be thought that chimpanzees, our nearest living relatives with whom we share 98.6 per cent of our DNA, represented creatures ancestral to ourselves, but we now realize that they have their own evolutionary paths, so that our joint ancestors have no living analogues. The date of the split between lineages leading to humans and apes is calculated on the basis of genetic divergence to be around 7 mya and the fossil record is scant for this period, with the exotically named *Sahelanthropus tchadensis* (found in Chad near a large, now-dry lake) and the slightly later *Orrorin tugensis* (found in the Tugen Hills, Kenya) being the earliest known so far (Figure 2). What marks these species as human ancestors is an upright stance for walking on the ground, rather than living in trees.

We are not sure what relationship these early species had to humans today. The species most likely to be directly ancestral to ourselves is *Ardipithecus ramidus* (known colloquially as Ardi) dating to 4.4 mya. We are now in the Pliocene (5.3–2.6 mya), when the earth's climate cooled towards the last glaciation. Tectonically significant effects occurred—North and South America joined when the Caribbean plate shifted west; India made contact with Asia initiating the Himalayas, and the African plate pushing into Europe started to uplift the Alps, so that eventually a band of mountains came into being from France to Sichuan. The Mediterranean Sea dried up completely, becoming plains with grasslands. Cooling led to ice forming at both poles. The increase in grasslands, which started in the Miocene, continued.

The professional and popular conception is that human evolution unfolded on the grassland savannah of east Africa. A near complete skeleton of Ardi has been found in Ethiopia, an adult female 1.2 metres (almost 4 feet) tall with a brain of 325 cc

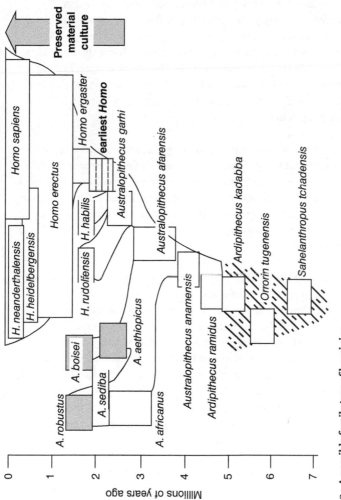

2. A possible family tree of hominins.

(cubic capacity). Surprisingly, as indicated by the animal species found with her, Ardi lived not on the savannah, but in dense woodland with open patches here and there. She was an omnivore, not yet concentrating on the seeds, roots, and animal protein of the savannah, seen with later hominin species. An apparently insignificant aspect of Ardi's body may be important: her canine teeth are much smaller than those of apes, hinting that she may have done more with her hands, and also that the lesser weight of teeth made it easier to balance her head on a more upright spine.

After Ardi we encounter a plethora of species, which bring with them terminological and intellectual confusion. First is the term hominin, which might look like a misprint. Hominid is now used to group our lineage with those of the gorilla and chimpanzee, in distinction to the orang-utan, a more distant cousin. Consequently, hominin now designates all species thought to be directly related to ourselves.

The most accepted direct ancestors to modern humans are the Australopethicines, of whom there were many long-lived species, indicating how successful they were in evolutionary terms. The earliest, *Australopithecus anamensis*, may appear around 4 mya, either deriving from Ardi or living in parallel with her—we cannot tell between these two alternatives. By 3 mya Australopethicines are found from the southern tip of Africa north to Ethiopia and at least as far west as Chad. We are dealing with a few hundred specimens at best, many of which are only known from a few bones, with the contexts varying between secure to more or less disturbed. Added to this, various specialists differ on the criteria for classifying these creatures and on the behavioural implications of bodily characteristics. Some people are lumpers, preferring a few species within which it is accepted there will be variation, and others are splitters, who feel that the recognition and designation of variety is important to understand evolutionary processes.

A crucial characteristic of all Australopethicines is that the hind limb has given up grasping and is fully adapted to walking on the ground. A poignant testimony to walking are the footprints made by two adults and a child walking across fresh volcanic ash at Laetoli, Tanzania, between 3.8 and 3.5 mya, with the tracks of other animals. The child and an adult walk together: it is possible the child was holding the adult's hand (Figure 3).

Whatever we think about the range and number of species, it is clear that there were both robust and gracile Australopethicines. The former group includes *Australopithecus robustus*, *boisei*, and *aethipiopicus* (all seen by some as a separate genus *Paranthropus*) and the latter group includes *Australopithecus anamensis*, *africanus*, *afarensis*, *garhi*, and *sediba* at a minimum. The robust group has larger teeth, the graciles a bigger brain.

With the head perched on top of the spine, an evolutionary choice is necessary between large brain and big teeth; both would create too much weight. We, with our extraordinarily large brains (at 1,350 cc almost three times the weight of an Australopethicine brain), see that the correct evolutionary route was taken by the graciles. The best-known Australopethicine skeleton is that known as Lucy from the Hadar area of Ethiopia, with relatively well-preserved fossils and the site of high-quality work by an Ethiopian and American team.

From possibly around 2.4 mya the first members of the early *Homo* genus appear in east Africa. The dividing line between Australopethicines and humans is brain size, although there is considerable variation in the brains of both taxa. *Homo habilis* had a brain size of some 650 cc, larger than most Australopethicines, but considerably smaller than later *Homo ergaster*. Between around 2.4 and 1.5 mya in eastern and southern Africa (and maybe elsewhere) was found an extraordinary range of genera and species in the hominin lineage, some of which must have interacted with others in ways we cannot now imagine.

3. The Laetoli footprints.

The big development in this period is the first stone tools
at around 2.6 mya, with chopper tools and flakes, crude by
later standards but beyond what any chimpanzee can produce
today. Tools with regular flakes are testimony to fine motor

control in the hand of their maker, as well as the ability to foresee a desired outcome. It was thought, due to rather self-reinforcing reasoning, that it was *Homo* that produced and used tools. Indeed *Homo habilis* translates as handy man. Tools now predate *Homo*, although this could just be an accident of the state of our discoveries. But no direct evidence for who did what exists and it is quite possible that the gracile Australopethicines made up for the loss of cutting and ripping front teeth through the use of stones to grind, mash, and otherwise process plant remains and perhaps to butcher scavenged animals.

A larger brain is hungry for protein, which might have spurred a move from plant foods to meat, although hunting seems unlikely at this early period. Good stone for making tools was moved over tens of kilometres on occasion, indicating both a recognition of the outcrops with the best flaking properties and a degree of planning and forethought. Large brains did not just enable keener thought about physical properties of things, but also allowed more complex sociability, and it is possible that both Australopethicines and early humans lived in larger and more complicated groups than hitherto. The development of material and social life went hand in hand.

All our evidence for human evolution prior to 1.8 mya is restricted to Africa. We are now in the Pleistocene (2.6 mya–11.7 kya), the Ice Age period. Terminological confusion is possible here. The Pleistocene is a geological period, like the Miocene and Pliocene, defined in terms of the world's climate, flora, fauna, and positions of the continents. An archaeological period, the Palaeolithic, runs from the start of human origins through to the start of the modern era, the geological period of the Holocene (11.7 kya to the present). Certainly in archaeology we are saddled with periods deriving from the Victorian era that are no longer helpful or clearly defined, but are in such common use that it is hard to do away with them.

Out of Africa

The first hominin to leave Africa was probably *Homo erectus* around 1.8 mya. Big claims are made for this species, but there is still surprising uncertainty surrounding it. As Robin Dennell points out some of the earliest dates for *erectus* may be from Dmanisi in Georgia (although here it has been called *Homo georgicus*), with early finds as far afield as Java. Dennell floats the idea that earlier species, possibly even Australopethicines, may have left Africa, as there were periods when there were no ecological barriers to exit. These groups might have evolved further outside of Africa, so that *erectus* might have moved into Africa from Asia and not the other way round. Given the widespread distribution of *erectus*, it is not surprising that differences in body type, size, and shape are seen.

It is likely that *Homo erectus* originated that quintessential Palaeolithic artefact, the hand axe (hand axes first occur in Kenya and Ethiopia at least 1.75 mya and are still found some 150 kya, a life use of well over 1.5 million years). A hand axe is flaked on both sides to give sharp edges. It fits into the hand with a rounded butt and tapers to a point at the other end. Hand axes are perhaps 15 centimetres (6 inches) long and they weigh about the same as a small bag of sugar. Hand axes, to us at least, also have a beauty to them, exhibiting both left–right and front–back symmetry. There are occasions, for instance, at the famous site of Boxgrove, near Chichester in southern Britain, that hand axes appear to have been made and not used, and others which were used and then deposited together in large numbers in deliberate ways. East African sites evidence accumulations of hand axes. It might appear that there were rules of making and of use for hand axes that continued over huge lengths of time. Hand axes were made by both *Homo erectus* and a successor species, *Homo heidelbergensis*, with one material form spanning two species and probably being used in the same manner.

The first occupants of Europe around 1 mya were probably *Homo heidelbergensis*, who moved north during warmer periods, and this is a story we will pick up in the next chapter. *Homo heidelbergensis* may well also have been the common ancestor of Neanderthals and ourselves, with Neanderthals being more cold-adapted. Most people think that anatomically modern humans, *Homo sapiens sapiens*, first arose in Africa around 300 kya, but even here there is controversy. The recent African origin model (recent in evolutionary terms that is!) holds that everyone in the world today descends from a common ancestral group in Africa and spread a little less than 100 kya into the Middle East and thence into Europe, Asia, and beyond.

Modern humans encountered previous groups of humans, the best known of which are the Neanderthals (*Homo sapiens neanderthalensis*), found throughout Eurasia. After a period of considerable overlap, especially in areas like the Middle East and Europe, the Neanderthals died out (whether they were wiped out by our ancestors or could not survive in the same landscape as them is unknown but the subject of much speculation in TV programmes and novels), leaving us as the only hominin species for the first time.

The competing hypothesis, known as the multi-regional model, holds that modern humans derive ultimately from populations of *Homo erectus* which moved out of Africa from about 1.8 mya onwards into Europe (probably), Asia, and southeast Asia, down to places like present-day Java. This is much less likely.

Human genetic variability is very low, much less than that found within chimps or gorillas. The differences of skin colour, hair, and face shape, which some people make so much of, are controlled by very few genes and tend to mask a much deeper human unity. Equally important as evidence against the multi-regional hypothesis is the fact that the recovery of ancient DNA from three different Neanderthal skeletons in Europe and the Caucasus indicates no genetic link between ourselves and Neanderthals, making it very unlikely that they are the ancestors of present-day Europeans, all of whom derive from the African migrants, as must be true for the rest of the globe.

To complicate matters, later evidence shows some evidence of interbreeding between *neanderthals* and *sapiens*. Last, but by no means least, the earliest fossils of fully modern humans are found in Africa, only turning up later elsewhere, and this may also be true of some types of stone tools associated with our own direct ancestors. For most prehistorians, a recent African origin for fully modern humans is the only means to make sense of the evidence we have. One point to bear in mind, however, is that the greatest level of human genetic diversity in the world is found in west Africa. So that it may be the east-Africa-centred view of early evolution will eventually be seen as partial and influenced by the evidence we presently have available.

This brings us to the question of the nature of various hominins' lives and their engagement with each other, with other species, and with the broader material world.

Humans are symbiotic animals. This is interestingly true at the level of the microbiome, where roughly half the cells in our bodies are other organisms, as mapped by the recent Human Microbiome Project. Contemporary mapping showed the greatest diversity of organisms in the mouth and the gut, but also the degree to which these varied between individuals, parts of the world, and cultures arising from a complex interplay of genes and environmental factors. Humans also enter symbiotic relations with larger species, typically plants and animals. Many other species have a range of long-term symbiotic relations, which may affect the evolution of each, such as the relationship between flowering plants and bees which aid in pollination. More unusual examples are those of the clown fish and Ritteri sea anemones in which the fish protects the anemone from other fish who might eat it and the stinging tentacles of the anemone protects the clown fish from its predators.

Human symbiosis has two unusual features compared with the biological world more broadly. We enter into a great range of symbiotic relations with many different species, and this includes not just the major domesticates found across the world, but also species like gazelle and reindeer which were technically wild, or only partly domesticated. Second, from at least the late Palaeolithic onwards, but probably before, symbiosis involves material culture, whether this be hunting weapons, hides, and drives for animals, but also the creation of beneficial environments for plants (which much later come to be called fields) through various forms of landscape alteration.

I'm raising the issue of symbiosis here, as there is a further evolutionary point when we are looking at a range of hominins living together, or in close proximity. We have tended to assume that relations between Australopithecines and early *homo* or (more particularly) between *Homo sapiens* and Neanderthals were always antagonistic, driven by competition. We should entertain the possibility that symbiotic relations may also have existed between earlier hominins, whose actions may have reinforced the mosaic nature of habitats in places like east Africa, so that one species helped another thrive, probably accidentally rather than through any design.

There is a broader point here. The fact of evolution is not at all controversial within the scholarly community. However, there is discussion as to how evolution takes place. The Darwinian model encoded competition into the heart of evolutionary theory, through the phrase 'the survival of the fittest'. Competition is a partial driver of evolution, but more complementary, symbiotic relations are increasingly seen as important. In addition, the flow of genes between species, through the action of the microbiome, is recognized as small-scale, fast-acting, and cumulatively influential.

Lastly, the relationships between genes and the broader environment are complicating earlier ideas, so that why genes are activated under varying environmental conditions is increasingly of interest. Biology, like many other disciplines, is embracing complexity and relationships; evolution happens through the ecosystem as a whole and not in isolated organisms, and relations of the ecosystem include beneficial relations as well as antagonistic ones. Human evolution is of great concern to us, so that, despite its patchy evidence, it forms an excellent case study through which to approach broader questions of evolution and the particularities of human change and development. I will return to issues of symbiosis in the chapters to come.

The hardest, but most interesting, questions of the Palaeolithic concern the intelligence and sociability of hominins. We should not see early genera and species as displaying unformed or primitive versions of contemporary human lives. From the Australopithecines onwards these creatures developed their own forms of life. In Chapter 2, I argued that it was the triangular relationship between brain, body, and world that make us human. The further back we go, the more difference exists in all three elements. We have seen that the shape of the world in the Pliocene was unlike today; hominin's bodies were smaller, as were their brains; tool use also looked quite different. These were social primates, however, with a depth of relationship with things not exhibited by any other primate today, and with modes of communication which did not include language, but might have been sophisticated in many ways.

Joint attention and joint intention are two important dimensions of these emerging worlds. From the age of around 9 months a human infant can look at an adult pointing to something and take in both the human gesture and the object of interest, making some deductions about what the adult is interested in and why it might be interesting. Humans are also able to share the attention of another species. If we know an animal well we can have some sense of what worries, excites, or causes them fear, and react accordingly. Sharing the attention of another is a vital building block of social life, leading on to a further element which is joint intention, where two or more people can share a purpose for anything from minutes to years. This can also transfer from people to other species, such as when an ox ploughs a field or a dog hunts with people.

A common purpose is powerful, developing slowly among our ancestors over millions of years of human evolution, but it is hard to find direct evidence for. A large recent project on the social brain by Clive Gamble, John Gowlett, and Robin Dunbar provides important new insights into these complex areas (see Further Reading). They start with a contrast between primate sociability, mainly established through grooming, and that of humans in which language and complex material culture are crucial.

Grooming can only take place between individuals, but language connects a much larger group. Material culture also lays down rules of making and acting. The very specific form of a hand axe can only be arrived at through using fine-grained rock and removing particular flakes in the right sequence. Large accumulations of hand axes in east Africa and elsewhere are mysterious, but are evidence of broadly shared intention and attention. A well-coordinated group is essential for activities like hunting, where stealth, speed, and patience must all be shared across a group. Chimpanzees have occasionally been seen to hunt things like lizards using sticks as rudimentary spears.

The fact that hominins increased and spread across the world almost 2 mya indicates that they were not battling for survival and that their lives were made up of a novel breadth and depth of sociability. Shared intentions across some tens of individuals became possible and links between groups are hinted at from the movement of raw materials for hand axes of up to 100 kilometres (60 miles) from Gadeb in Ethiopia 1 mya. By the middle

Palaeolithic, after 800 kya, such distances become commonplace and are often exceeded.

We share our intentions in and through artefacts. A spear is a relatively simple artefact in some ways: a long, thin piece of wood that has been shaped. Making a spear requires judgement about length, thickness, balance, and the type of wood used. The maker has to anticipate the flight of the spear when thrown, the effectiveness of its point in piercing the hide of prey, and so on. Very different judgements and anticipations are needed when making a hand axe or any other artefact.

Only humans can make and control fire. Fire occurs naturally, through lightening strikes and other means, and can then be harvested by hominins. The very long history of fire runs from making use of natural bushfires to regularly making and feeding fire in a controlled manner, through the use of hearths. Gorillas, chimps, and orang-utans all eat hundreds of different plants in the relatively wet and lush habitats they generally inhabit, and chimpanzees will occasionally supplement plant food with insects, honey, and hunted lizards or even small mammals. There is a theory that the dry-country apes who were our ancestors could only survive on the savannah through eating novel foods, such as tubers and more meat. Both tubers and meat can be hard for the human gut to digest in a raw state. Following this logic, some use of fire would have been a necessary precondition for successful savannah living.

The flaw to an argument of this kind is that we have no direct evidence of the controlled use of fire from the earliest period of savannah life. The first convincing evidence of the controlled use of fire comes from two South African caves—Swartkrans and Wonderwerk—which have levels of many burnt bones between 800 kya and 1 mya. In earlier levels in these caves are the remains of Australopithecines who might have been dragged in there as the food of large predators. Safe living in caves for later hominins might have been enabled by fire. Scaring large fierce animals is just one limited use of fire, which could also extend the social day into the hours of darkness (human patterns of sleep are much briefer than those of apes, maybe as a result of a long history of staying awake after dark), cooking food, working on materials—through the hardening of spear tips or making stone easier to flake, but also due to the burning of vegetation to encourage the growth of young, edible shoots as opposed to more woody, older plant growth. It is hard to overestimate the consequences of controlled fire making and use, not least because it was vital in movements into more northerly, colder latitudes.

Gamble and colleagues see a marked growth in the brain of *Homo heidelbergensis* from around 600 kya and this might indicate some form of language, which probably was not fully syntactical, but might have included a range of sounds and gestures, using as well the qualities of artefacts like hand axes in various forms of expression. Language, in whatever form, is important for generating and sustaining joint attention and intentions. *Homo heidelbergensis* probably made the first composite tools of stone and wood, combining materials with varied sources and properties, commonplace today but life changing when first done.

The first wooden tools are known from Israel around 700 kya, although it is almost certain they existed earlier and we lack evidence. There is a spectrum in the likelihood of various technologies to survive, with stone resisting erosion or decay, clay also survives when dried or fired, but basketry, fibres, nets, and so on are all very unlikely to be preserved. It is only with the upper Palaeolithic from around 20 kya that we gain indications of organic technologies, although they must have developed over much longer periods.

A vital element of hominin life is the history of clothing. The hair-covered hominins living in warm climates could survive without clothes, covering, or shelter. But as soon as they moved into areas that were seasonally chilly or cold at night, some protection was needed. Again, we can be sure that by the upper Palaeolithic, when humans are found in very cold environments, clothes were varied and sophisticated. The existence of bone pins and needles indicate that sewing, presumably mainly of skins, but possibly also of plant fibres, was frequent and skilled. The deeper history of clothing is important to understand, but hard to give substance to at present.

It seems likely that *Homo heidelbergensis* hunted. From this broad period onwards camp sites show more activities around a central hearth, with considered deposition of rubbish. It might be that we can trace many of the elements of what makes us human back to the start of the middle Palaeolithic, even among creatures that were not identical to us in physical form.

The African evidence over seven million years is puzzling, intriguing, and confronting. It is a massive understatement to say much more remains to be learned. Only in eastern and southern Africa have there been concerted programmes of research on early human evolution and even here large areas are little known. Much of the African continent has been little researched for these very early periods, even though there are hints that discoveries await which will overturn our current picture. The Miocene history of hominins is especially thin, and we know little about the range of creatures that existed in the late Miocene and early Pliocene, from 3.5 to 2 mya. Our ancestors then have been called 'dry-country apes' and the feeling has been that it was the expanding savannah grasslands that provided the locus for hominin lives and evolution.

This is partly true, but as both the animals found with hominin skeletons and the range of physical types of early Australopithecines show, it is likely that a range of habitats from woodland to grassland were used, with creatures perhaps moving between them. Quite what the relations were between various hominin species and

40

genera is unknown and has been given little thought, but is intriguing. The interactions between types of hominin might have been an important spur to the evolution of all and could have been cooperative, or mutually supporting, as well as competitive.

We do not know which creatures made and used the earliest stone tools and it is quite likely that Australopithecines as well as Homo were tool makers and users. *Homo erectus* at present seems a central link between the early, very diverse hominin world and a later situation of fewer species, with movements out of Africa across Eurasia. But much about *erectus* is in doubt, including whether it did arise in Africa or was Asian-born, perhaps deriving from earlier out of Africa movements which we have not yet spotted. Again whether it was restricted to the savannah in Africa seems unlikely, given the range of habitats colonized down to Java. The deep human story obviously starts in Africa, but it is possible that hominins could have migrated back into Africa, as well as out. We can see at the moment a line of descent from *erectus* to *heidelbergensis* to *Homo sapiens neanderthalensis* and *Homo sapiens sapiens*, but this might be too simple or simply wrong.

We are inclined to view many elements of our later human story as arising around the start of the middle Palaeolithic some 800 kya, which could include some form of language, more organized sites, the use of fire, clothing, and longer-distance movement of stone and composite technologies. Together these seem to show a greater depth of creation of local places than hitherto within a much greater spatial compass, in turn indicating enhanced appreciations of time and space.

I shall now turn to Europe and Asia, looking first at their early human history before concentrating on the dramatic changes that occur at the end of the last glacial.

Chapter 4
The long-term history of Europe and Asia

The ice ages

From around 2.3 mya, relatively minor changes in the earth's orbit, spin, and tilt caused the climate to fluctuate between warm and cold periods, affected also by how the newly formed Himalayas and Tibetan Plateau influenced global circulation systems. The amplitude of the climatic cycles increased over time and the difference between the coldest and warmest periods heightened. Fluctuating climatic systems provide the context in which the global expansion of our ancestors occurred and there is no reason to think that climatic fluctuations have ceased. We can see some forty-one cycles of cold and warm periods of varying lengths, which now provide the climatic and ecological framework for Palaeolithic archaeology.

Let us focus on one recurring ecosystem: that known as the mammoth steppe. From around 478 to 427 kya large carnivores declined in relative numbers and a set of cold steppe ecosystems came into being, with mammoths, woolly rhinos, and reindeer as the most common large mammals—these ecosystems are now known by the shorthand of the mammoth steppe. These were all grazing animals that ate a variety of plants, which helped them survive in the range of conditions that came to exist across Europe.

The mammoth steppe existed in cold periods for almost half a million years and with each warming the cold-loving plants and animals were driven to the tundra regions to the east and north, recolonizing a huge swathe of Eurasia and Alaska with each downturn in temperature. An upswing of the temperature saw pulses of warm-loving ecosystems colonizing from the south then erased again, except for relatively small refuge areas, as the ice sheets and tundra moved in from the north. Each iteration of the cold- and warm-loving ecosystems were broadly similar, but never quite the same. Both cold- and warm-adapted communities have no modern analogues. Until around 100 kya hominins (Neanderthals) were part of the warm-adapted communities, although the range of environments and climates in which they could live increased over time.

Not only did communities of plants and animals fluctuate, but the surface of the earth was radically transformed. The ice sheets from almost half a million years ago, for instance, pushed major river systems, such as the Thames and the Seine, to the south, close to their present positions. From this period on major depositions of loess occurred across Eurasia to become the focus, many millennia later, of intense agricultural systems from central Europe to China. The Palaeolithic archaeologist, Clive Gamble, calls this period 'the hinge' partly because the evidence comes into new focus through extensive correlations of stratigraphy and fauna, in which small fast-evolving creatures, like voles, are key to understanding dates and temperatures.

For a long period hominins were part of the warm-adapted plant and animal communities. From around 500 kya there was probably a thin, but even, distribution of hominins across all areas of Europe, apart from the northeast, making hand axes and other flaked stone tools. These creatures were large, like the 1.8-metre-tall *Homo heidelbergensis*, and they lived in local groups without wide connections, as shown by the distances which raw materials traveled from their source (30–80 kilometres). Against the background of the long cycle of climates and ecosystems startling snapshots stand out, such as the knapping (i.e. production of stone tools through removing flakes) episodes to produce bifaces (i.e. tools with a defined front and back) at the site of Boxgrove, near Chichester, southern England. Here blocks of stone can be fitted back together to show how knapping took place a few hundred metres from where the stone was procured, with the hand axes then being used to butcher animal carcasses on these tidal flats before being discarded.

Wooden tools are also known from a number of middle Pleistocene locations, the most remarkable of which is Schöningen in eastern Germany, where throwing and thrusting spears have been found, one of which may have had a hafting for a stone tool. Many were deposited in peats while still in serviceable condition, raising the question of why, like hand axes, they should have been discarded in that particular location and time? The tips of some spears were also made from the hard heartwood of spruce, showing a considerable appreciation for the variability and properties of materials.

The broader ecological situation of all our remote ancestors is only partly clear. We do not know with certainty whether early hominins lived in Europe only in warm periods, or also in cold. Some of the oldest evidence in Britain and indeed in Europe, from Happisburgh, Norfolk over 800 kya appears to come from a period with wooded conditions equivalent to that found in southern Scandinavia today, raising questions about hominin survival in the deep winter if they did not have clothing, shelter, or fire.

Adaptation to local ecological conditions is one question. How far our ancestors linked with each other across space is also important. From the relatively face-to-face social encounters at Boxgrove and before, there is evidence that materials for tools moved over much longer distances from the late Middle

Palaeolithic onwards, and by the Upper Palaeolithic movements of up to 200 kilometres are common. In all cases of long-distance movements only small amounts of stone were moved and these were used up in the process of making stone tools. There is also a shift from bifaces and flakes to blades (blades are more than twice as long as they are wide).

An interestingly complicating factor in relatively new evidence of the last glaciation is for a variety of hominin species, which now include the so-called Denisovans excavated in a cave in eastern Siberia that I have been lucky enough to visit. Analysis of the genetics of bones and teeth, show that Denisovans had genetic links with Neanderthals and other archaic forms of Homo, as well as passing their genes, through migration, to populations in Australia and Melanesia.

Not far from northern Australia, on Flores in the Indonesian island chain, come fossils from the diminutive *Homo floresiensis*, which might date back some 200,000 years until around 22 kya. Now known to the world as the 'hobbit', these creatures are puzzling because of their small stature and brains, although they did use stone tools. Debate is still underway as to whether the 'hobbits' became small through living on an island, as is known for dwarf forms of animals, or if they were of that stature when they arrived. The latter possibility makes it likely that there are lineages out there of which we presently know nothing. Alternatively, the 'hobbit' might have gained its characteristics through some unknown pathology. The stark nature of these alternatives demonstrates how much is still to be learned about even relatively recent human history.

It used to be thought that the Upper Palaeolithic (*c.*40–10 kya) was a period of revolution, an important precursor for the Neolithic revolution that occurred after global warming. People like Richard Klein have argued strongly, using multiple lines of evidence, for rapid change around 50–40 kya, which included a growth in the range and standardization of artefact types that changed more rapidly than previously, creating regionally distinct sets of artefacts: the first use of materials like bone and shell for points, awls, needles, and pins; the earliest true art; well-organized camp sites, including well-built hearths with activities organized around these; movement of raw materials, especially stone, over hundreds of kilometres; evidence for ritual both through art and burial; the first habitation of the very coldest parts of Eurasia; higher population densities than previously; the first fishing. Maybe, it was thought, these traits emerged as a rather late result of becoming anatomically modern, attaining the bodies we have today.

More interestingly, people like Stephen Mithen argued that it was the growth in symbolism that allowed for rapid change. The definition of a symbol is 'something that stands for something else'—the colour red for blood; or the word 'cat' for the animal. Ivory and bone are carved into the shapes of people and animals and so-called Venus figurines are made from clay and stone. The Sunghir necklace, found on a site in northern Russia at the height of the last glacial (around 18 kya), was made from 3,000 individual beads, and must have enhanced or changed the social standing of the wearer in some manner (Figure 4). Symbolic linkages allow for creativity through connecting different elements of the material world.

Language is also a part of these debates. Tool use is characteristic of humanity, although we now know that many other creatures make and use tools. Tool-using people can complement these skills with that of language. There is considerable controversy as to when human language started, whether with the Neanderthals (or even earlier) or with the fully moderns. Attempts to teach chimpanzees to speak in the 1960s foundered on the fact that chimps lack the right architecture of the mouth and throat to create the range of sounds that we can. They were unable to speak at all well.

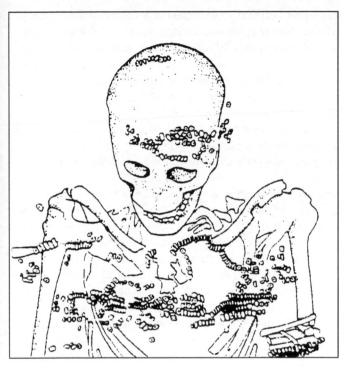

4. The Sunghir burial with necklace.

Once the researchers switched to sign language, however, things changed, so that both chimps and gorillas were able to demonstrate sophisticated concepts about themselves, others, the material world, the past, and the future through signing.

Much discussion of Neanderthal language concerned whether they could vocalize in the same manner as ourselves, a discussion held back by the lack of direct evidence on their throat length, tongue, or palate. Even if they could not speak, Neanderthals could probably communicate through a combination of actions and sounds. But the question turns not only on physical abilities, but also on social needs.

The longer, deeper chains of action involving extended and deep relations between people and things over time and space seem to be lacking for the Middle Palaeolithic. Neanderthal societies, for whatever reason, restrained the need to develop sophisticated forms of linguistic communication. Neanderthals may not have felt the need to engage in discussions of the type of 'Remember that mammoth we killed five years ago, I'm still using one of its bones to knap flint with', whereas a fully modern human might have said 'I treasure this bow, because it was made for me by my mother using the sinews of a mammoth she helped kill five years ago'.

Of course we will never know the emotional attachments of either species but we suspect a greater range and depth of attachments to people and things from the Upper Palaeolithic than for any previous period, and a greater ability to express these attachments verbally. Deep attachments to artefacts and to people derived both from the things themselves and their significances, but also from words spoken about people and things. This sets up a tension between the habitual, taken-for-granted areas of life, which we feel but cannot speak, and words which directly, if only partially, express what people feel. It is this tension between words and action that is crucial to our lives and may not have existed for any other species.

The upper Palaeolithic, as Clive Gamble has written, involved 'the Other becoming Us'. Gamble feels that the main change is not so much a revolution as a growing freedom from the immediacies of life, so that time and space become socially extended. Boxgrove hominids made beautiful hand axes, demonstrating considerable skill in producing artefacts of great utility and considerable aesthetic appeal (to us and possibly to them). These hand axes were made from material obtained locally and were often dropped very close to where they had been used.

In the Upper Palaeolithic artefacts take on significances beyond the here and now, extending people's chains of social connection over space and across time. Material culture and social relations are intimately linked, so that one could not exist in the same form without the other. Places and people were probably imbued with meanings and emotional responses as never before. Workers looking at the African evidence are now insisting that many of the innovations attributed as new to the Upper Palaeolithic derive from the Middle Palaeolithic, giving us a much more continuous prehistory.

This is the view I feel sympathy with and we can extend it by saying that many developments attributed to the first farmers derive from the Upper Palaeolithic. These include (partly) sedentary life, querns, pestles, and mortars for processing wild grasses and nuts, as well as pottery.

Food and long-term continuity

Part of the classic story of the Neolithic is that pottery was invented by the first farmers in the Middle East and taken by migrant agriculturalists to places like Europe. We now know that this is not true: pottery was invented by Palaeolithic groups independently in both east Asia (maybe 20 kya at Xianrendong Cave in southern China) and north Africa (by 14 kya—various sites in Mali, Tunisia, and the Nile Valley). It seems possible that pots diffused across Eurasia along a band of ecosystems that then had flora and fauna similar to the Mediterranean. Pots were accepted into hunter-gatherer societies in places like Scandinavia from groups to the east—it used to be thought that it was only with the movement of farmers that northern European hunter-gatherers gained pots. More controversially, it is probable that pots entered the Near East from African hunter-gatherer groups. Apart from anything else, this reverses what is seen as the normal flow of cultural influence, which is from a superior farming lifestyle to an evolutionarily earlier hunter-gatherer one.

Unsurprisingly, influence flowed in both directions. Early pots made cooking over a fire and storage easier, but were used for different things in various areas. The southern Chinese pottery is the earliest known example of the widespread occurrence of pottery across China, Japan, and eastern Russia. Looking at residues on the insides of pots, it is possible to say that many of these eastern pots were used for boiling nuts (in China acorns seem especially popular), whereas some coastal Japanese communities boiled seafood too. The north African cooking in pots involved wild grasses, probably boiled into porridge or gruel, while in the Near East and Europe the storage and drinking of milk products was found. In all cases, however, more work is needed to give us a broader basis for conclusions about pottery use.

Pottery and cuisine are basic to cultural forms in many parts of the world, and in a provocative article Dorian Fuller and Mike Rowlands have argued that differences in early pottery use indicate extremely long-lasting attitudes not just to food, but to commensality and ritual. They argue that there is much more to food than calories and that we should switch from notions of subsistence to an interest in meals as cultural elements. Fuller and Rowlands make a broad distinction between boiling and roasting cultures.

In the east, early pottery was developed, perhaps from clay-lined baskets, in order to boil foods such as nuts (acorns need several days of processing to make them edible and healthy, including leaching in water, grinding, and boiling). In the Middle East, far to the west, grinding and roasting of wild grasses, such as wild emmer, wild barley, and small-seeded grasses, as well as acorns, might go back 23,000 years on the evidence of grinding technologies at sites like Ohalo II, a waterlogged site in the Sea of Galilee, with structures like houses, storage pits, and stone grinders. Such early culinary emphasis led eventually to the domestication of grasses and the baking of bread. In Asia, there were slow moves to domesticate rice through the early Holocene, in part, maybe, because this could be boiled and eventually replaced the emphasis on nuts.

They further argue that the ritual systems of the east revolve around the steam rising from a boiling pot as a means of connecting with the ancestors, as well as the much later Bronze Age proliferation of bronze ritual vessels for containing and heating liquids. In the west, through to at least the classical Greeks and Romans, the offering of roast meat to the gods and the smoke ascending to heaven is crucial and possibly has Palaeolithic roots. This last point is crucial, as it provides for a very different chronology and sense of history than that of the Neolithic Revolution. The Neolithic, it used to be thought, created a massive break from what happened before and set the foundation for contemporary settled, agrarian lifestyles. If Fuller and Rowlands' argument has merit, then we can see moves towards farming, which are in any case slow, derived from cultural forms developed at least in the last glacial by hunter-gatherer groups and maybe earlier. Farming developed out of a continuity of cultural practices, as well as changes in them.

Let us now look at the slow moves towards farming starting in the Palaeolithic, first considering the Middle East, and then China and the Far East. Let us start at a slightly arbitrary point, because the evidence comes into focus then, not necessarily because it marks an important departure, with the site of Ohalo II just mentioned.

Around 23 kya people lived in this spot for a millennium or so, in houses made of tamarisk, oak, and willow (all recovered because the site is waterlogged), at least during the spring and autumn as indicated by the plants and animals at the site. There was a great variety of environments nearby including savannah, steppe, woodland, and upland from which people hunted three species of gazelle (each with their own preferred habitat), goats, steppe ass, as well as aurochs (a large wild cow) and boar that lived in woodland, but they also fished or caught birds on the lake. There was a great range of plant foods—up to forty in all—including, as we have seen, wild wheat and barley, which were roasted, as well as wild olives and grapes, so important in their much later domesticated forms. We have evidence for partly settled life intermittently thereafter.

From 14 kya, centred between the Jordan Valley and the Mediterranean coast, are the groups now known as Natufians, with similar sites further north in Syria. They made reaping knives that show microscopic traces of polish from slicing through stems of plants such as wild grasses. The Natufians built small, round huts and may have lived in their sites all year as indicated by small pits, lined with stones or mud, in which they stored food. These modest features indicate an important change in attitudes to food away from the immediate consumption of plants and animals and towards delayed return. Once again this is the earliest evidence we have and it may be that people had previously been keeping cereals, legumes, and possibly meat through smoking, drying, salting, and storing in baskets or granaries.

Natufians hunted gazelle in large numbers and a range of large animals, but also smaller species, which might indicate the use of traps and nets. The largest settlements, like Ain Mallaha in Israel, might have housed up to 200 people, with the burial of the dead a further indication of permanency. These burials show body ornaments of stone and bone, but also shells brought in from the Mediterranean, Red Sea, and the Nile, along with tiny amounts of volcanic glass (obsidian) from Anatolia.

The Natufian started in a period of warmer and wetter climate at the end of the glacial, but suffered the downturn of the so-called Younger Dryas, which was cold and dry. Some groups probably went back to a mobile lifestyle, making some burials in older sedentary settlements. Elaborate burials are found at the end of the Natufian, which include a careful choice of animal species (one elderly woman was buried in the cave of Hilazon Tachtit, Galilee, with the tip of a golden eagle's wing, a severed human foot, fifty tortoises, an aurochs's tail, a leopard's pelvis, and other bones; this has been interpreted as the burial of a shaman).

In northern Syria on the middle Euphrates is a large lake behind a dam. Beneath the waters of the lake lies a site known as Abu Hureyra, excavated in the 1970s prior to the construction of the dam. The earliest phase of the site is contemporary with the Natufian presence further south, being first occupied some 13,500 years ago. The inhabitants of the site had access to a great range of foodstuffs and raw materials, including plants and animals from the wet valley of the Euphrates and a nearby wadi, those of the forest steppe, and slightly further away from the open-park woodland of the hills.

There are two superimposed settlements at Abu Hureyra; one in which people supplemented hunting and gathering with growing crops, and a later village where crops and domesticated animals became more important. In the earlier occupation, each spring herds of Persian gazelle moved north from their wintering grounds in southern Syria, through the El Kum pass, and on to the Euphrates. Abu Hureyra was sited just where they turned west to fan out across the steppe and the coming of the gazelle would have been the vital point in the inhabitants' lives for 2,000 years.

Over 150 plant species were collected, which included the systematic harvesting of wild einkorn (wheat) and barley, but also flavourings, medicines and dyes. Plants were extensively processed using querns and mortars, with women probably carrying out much of this work as shown by wear on joints. People's lives probably had a strong seasonal round. In April the coming of the gazelle herds would have meant an intensive period of slaughter, butchery, and possible salting or storage of some of the meat. This was also a time when many wild grasses needed to be gathered and by June rye needed harvesting. The onset of high summer between July and November meant there were millet and club-rush seeds to be gathered in the valley bottom and grasses, roots and tubers on the steppe, along with more casual hunting of deer and pigs. Between December and April roots and tubers were gathered and some hunting took place.

Settlement at Abu Hureyra existed between spring and late autumn, but may have been year round. Smaller groups would have gone off to camp sites to hunt or gather the plants occurring locally. Complex planning was needed through the annual cycle and across the varied habitats over steppe and valley (Figure 5). Once again sea shells, obsidian, and other exotics indicate longer-distance contacts.

At the start of the dryer, cooler conditions Abu Hureyra was abandoned, then reoccupied as a farming settlement after a break of some 2,000 years in the so-called Pre-Pottery Neolithic B (PPNB) phase. This is a confusingly named period, with two phases known as A (11.5–10.5 kya) and B (10.5–8.7 kya). The PPN groups were not initially farmers in any straightforward sense, despite the designation of Neolithic, and only become farmers in some areas in the latter phase. Sites vary in size and complexity, the most famous being Jericho, excavated by Kathleen Kenyon in the 1950s, which has a substantial stone wall that might have been used for defensive purposes, or perhaps to guard against floods. Like Natufian sites, those of the PPNA have round houses, storage pits, and burials, but are now regularly between 2,000 square metres and 3 hectares, as opposed to up to 1,000 square metres for Natufian sites.

One of the most striking discoveries in recent years has been at the site of Göbekli Tepe on a hill about 10 kilometres from the town of Urfa in southeastern Turkey. Partly cut into the underlying limestone are up to twenty-two circular features built around with stone walls, some of which also have benches. Most are yet to be excavated. Either set into the walls or free-standing in the middle of the structures are stone pillars up to 6 metres tall and maybe weighing 50 tonnes (Figure 6). These are by far the largest stone structures known in the world at the time.

Quarried locally and then dragged into place, the pillars were also carved to depict a variety of animals. The pillars are T-shaped, so that the horizontal element may represent a stylized human

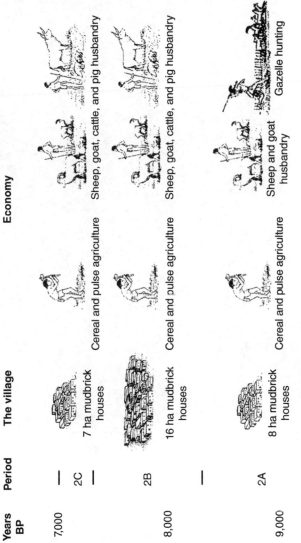

Years BP	Period	The village	Economy		
7,000	— 2C —	7 ha mudbrick houses	Cereal and pulse agriculture	Sheep, goat, cattle, and pig husbandry	
	2B	16 ha mudbrick houses	Cereal and pulse agriculture	Sheep, goat, cattle, and pig husbandry	
8,000	—				
9,000	2A	8 ha mudbrick houses	Cereal and pulse agriculture	Sheep and goat husbandry	 Gazelle hunting

5. **The chronology and activities at Abu Hureyra.**

6. The structures at Göbekli Tepe.

head, a conclusion strengthened by the existence of a face on one
pillar in Enclosure D and the fact that some have arms carved on
the longer sides, meeting as hands on the narrow face across,
in one case at least, a possible belt.

Göbekli Tepe is a site created by hunters and gatherers. Once again gazelle were a major prey animal, together with wild sheep, boar, and red deer. There is a considerable emphasis too on wild birds, including vultures, cranes, ducks, and geese, some of which may have been eaten, but which also carried a series of other values. Indeed many of the animals and birds carved on the pillars are predators or scavengers, perhaps carrying important associations for people who hunted themselves. People also gathered and processed wild cereals and there is evidence that this area of Turkey may have been home to the important wild wheats and barley that were later domesticated.

Around 5 per cent of Göbekli Tepe has been excavated, but so far there is no evidence of permanent habitation there. Currently it seems likely that occasional aggregations of people came here to feast, quarry, and carve pillars, later setting the latter into complex built structures. Once they had finished the use of a circle it was covered with a mound of feasting debris which had been curated nearby. Göbekli Tepe is always being interpreted in terms of their future: that it presaged later complex ritual lives, aggregation, and a concentration on some plants and animals later domesticated.

This was a future unknown to those who built Göbekli Tepe and, although they used plants later important to farmers, most of their animal protein came from the gazelle, which was never domesticated, and their images emphasize predatory animals and birds. Göbekli Tepe is best seen in its own right, as a centre for groups of people who negotiated significant relations with each other, stone, mud, animals, and plants. The site became historical, as the debris from past feasts accumulated over the stone circles on the hilltop, each newly built structure sitting near others which may have been centuries old. Stories and performances there would have taken in the old, new, and that to come. One possible recent discovery is that alcohol may have been brewed here to help give performances on the high hill a heightened emotional effect, but confirmation of this is needed.

Göbekli Tepe is remarkable, but is just one of a series of PPNA and PPNB sites found from Turkey, south through the Levant, with complex structures, sedentary life, and striking finds, such as human skulls with faces modelled in plaster, burials that combine human and animal bones into one composite skeleton, and continuing movement of materials, such as Red Sea shells, stone, and obsidian. By PPNB (10,500 to 8,700 years ago) the use of domesticated plants and animals had slowly evolved from their wild forms, with growing numbers of people in a single spot, now living in rectangular houses, as opposed to earlier round ones.

We can take again the site of Abu Hureyra as an example, occupied anew after a long hiatus. Houses were now constructed in mudbrick, with little space between them and on a layout, alignment, and form of construction that lasted for around 2,000 years. If a house was replaced every fifty years, this allows for some 400 replacements of houses in the life of the settlement. The settlement was now huge, covering some 16 hectares between 8.3 and 7.3 kya, housing between 5,000 and 6,000 people and requiring between 1,000 and 2,500 hectares of fields. There were now five domesticated cereals (rye, emmer, einkorn, and bread wheat, two- and six-hulled barley) and lentils, peas, and vetches, with field beans and chickpeas coming in after 7.3 kya.

Beneath the floors of the houses were human burials, with women more numerous than men. As in many sites of this age, emphasis was placed on the skull, which was often removed from the body and sometimes wrapped. Indeed, there is considerable evidence that burial was a final phase in an elaborate treatment of the body after death. Grave goods were often provided, including animal bones, bone beads, and obsidian, and such goods show no clear differences in gender.

Around 7 kya, pottery was introduced, which probably caused profound changes in the way in which food was prepared and served, as well as providing a very plastic medium for symbolism, through vessel shape and painting. House walls and floors were also painted, an activity which may have occurred regularly. Figurines of clay and stone were found in the shape of animals, as are common throughout southwest Asia.

The huge mudbrick village at Abu Hureyra is one of a large number of such early Neolithic communities found eventually from southeastern Europe across to central Asia. Each of these shares general common elements of architecture, pots, crops, and stone tools, but each region too has its own special ways of putting together the elements.

I excavated a small early Neolithic village in present-day Turkmenistan, at the base of the Iranian plateau and on the edge of the Kara Kum desert which stretches 1,000 kilometres to the north. Here was a small settlement of twenty to thirty houses in contemporary occupation, with beautiful painted pottery, an emphasis on einkorn as a crop, plus sheep and goat, but without any evidence of human burials. It is possible that, although the architecture of the site was permanent, the people in it were not, moving backwards and forwards between the lowland and the mountains, building and rebuilding their houses on a regular basis, so that the site built up rapidly with dates from the lowest and the highest houses indistinguishable at around 7 kya.

The Turkish site of Çatalhöyük, excavated currently by Ian Hodder and his team, is enormous in size and shows many of the elements of continuity found at Abu Hureyra, but has even more striking house decorations, artefacts, and burials. People established common cultures across Europe and Asia, but used commonalities in locally specific ways, responding to the needs and aspirations that they developed through new links between people, animals, plants, and the material world. Çatalhöyük was abandoned around 8 kya.

By this time people growing domesticated crops and animals were established in the Aegean, with similar groups starting to move through the Balkans. Across the Mediterranean people moved by sea, with sea faring another Palaeolithic innovation, built on further in the Neolithic and Bronze Ages.

Over many millennia, people, plants, and animals grew together in various ways: not invention so much as cohabitation in a situation of changing need. Jared Diamond has estimated that there are some 148 species of herbivores and omnivores worldwide that weigh 45 kilograms or more. Only fourteen of these species have been domesticated, leading us to wonder about the other 134 species. Even more surprising is that of the 200,000 higher plant species throughout the world, only around a hundred have been domesticated and used to any extent.

Despite recent massive research programmes spurred by modern agro-business, almost no extra species have been added to early rosters of food animals and plants. The vast majority of what we eat was domesticated in prehistory.

East Asian evidence

Another centre of experimentation, and eventually of domestication, was China. Here, as in Japan, Korea, and eastern Russia, trees were important. In some ways, long-term history over the past 20,000 years has seen a shift from a combination of nuts and grasses as staples, to various grasses which increased in importance—wheat, barley, oats, or rye in western Eurasia, rice in the east.

Late glacial relations with plants were influenced by the glacial cycle itself. Around 18 kya the vast landmass that is now China was cold and dry, and the sea level was 120 metres below the present, with Japan joined to the Sakhalin Peninsula in the north and very close to touching an expanded Chinese and Korean mainland further south. Along the Yellow River, artemisia (a pleasant-smelling herb) steppe and grasses were found, in the Yangtze valley to the south, stands of trees were found. By 12 kya, north, northeast, and central China were all wetter and warmer, with temperate forests expanding in the south out of sheltered refuges, lake levels rising, and the monsoon cycle starting to assert itself a few millennia later.

From over 20 kya both wild grasses and nuts were gathered and processed, with an emphasis on grass in the north and nuts in the south, but in both cases people developed a lifestyle in which they stayed in some sites for considerable parts of the year. Pottery is found sporadically across China through the late glacial, as we have seen, and its occurrence may have been more widespread than our present evidence suggests. As recent climatic conditions start to develop, people broaden their plant use to include beans, tubers, and nuts as well as grasses, so that Holocene ways of life develop directly from older forms.

Cave sites along the middle Yangtze and in Guangxi furnish most of the late glacial evidence from southern China, with striking evidence for the earliest pottery in the world. Pots may have been used for cooking wild rice as well as nuts. Fish, shellfish, deer, wild pig, and water buffalo were also eaten. By the earliest Holocene, the initial layers of sites like Shangsan (11.4–8.6 kya) show complex grinding stones, pottery, storage pits, the careful dumping of domestic refuse, and possible wooden pile dwellings which all indicate a sedentary lifestyle based on wild foods, by part of the population at least. Echoes of Natufian and PPNA sites are unmistakable. Complex settlements are also found in Japan, where the Jomon culture lasts for most of the Holocene, initially based on wild food and with a later mixture of wild and domesticated foodstuffs.

Much research has gone into the understanding of the domestication of rice. This is partly because of its importance today, but also due to difficulties in defining criteria to divide domesticated from wild rice. Most researchers agree that there were several thousand years between the use of wild rice at the end of the Pleistocene and the development of fully domesticated rice by the middle of the Holocene. For most of this period, rice was one component of a broad range of plant use, which included also millets, soybean, and tubers.

Tubers were part of southern, tropical modes of subsistence that were found down through southeast Asia to Papua New Guinea, including taro and various forms of yam. Millet, in its two forms of foxtail and broomcorn millet, was probably domesticated in northern China and wild forms are known to have been used from the late Pleistocene onwards, providing reasonable yields even before cultivation or domestication. Soybean may well have been domesticated in the late Holocene independently in the Yellow River, Korea, and Japan. By this time wheat, barley, and oats had already been introduced from the west. Anyone visiting China today will be impressed by the range of food on the table, especially of plants. There are long histories behind this variety stretching back to the late glacial and involving plants and animals brought in from the tropics or from the steppe to the west.

Towards a new model

An emphasis on the origins of farming has given us a two-phase view of history: a before when everyone was hunter-gatherers and an after with domesticated plants and animals, sedentary life, crafts such as pottery, and moves towards more complex social relations. Accumulating evidence from across the planet looks very different. From at least the late glacial onwards, over the last 20 kya or so, people have experimented with plants and animals, so that many crops later cultivated were harvested in wild form and maybe cultivated. Trees were important, as they continued to be over the last 10,000 years, but were increasingly displaced by cereals and root crops. Pottery was a Pleistocene invention, as was seafaring in the Mediterranean, Indian Ocean, and Near Oceania. The dog was domesticated from the grey wolf somewhere in the north of the planet. People had close relations with other species such as gazelle or reindeer, the former as a hunted wild animal and the reindeer in both domesticated and wild forms.

Late Pleistocene ways of life were not just a series of isolated experiments, but were centred on connected practices that might have huge longevity. Cooking, which focused on steaming and boiling in the east, was not just about what was culturally acceptable food, although this was important, but linked also to ritual practices and connections to powers beyond the human. Bread was the stuff of life in the Judeo-Christian tradition, which probably has very ancient roots, through grains as foodstuff but also a set of cultural associations. People do not live by bread alone (although it is often hard to live without it), but through links with cosmological powers. The massive structures found at Göbekli Tepe show a commitment to quarrying, carving, and setting stones of many tonnes in built circular settings. But rather than slavishly following sets of orthodox beliefs, people are better seen as engaging in sets of experiments concerning food, social relations, and cosmology.

People had a range of significant relations across the planet with other living species, but also with stone, clay, and later metal, which were conceived of not just in functional terms—questioning how best to make a living—but also through relationships conceived of in a rounded manner. The development of a new relationship with early domesticated dogs or clay fired as pots was also a development of the skills of the human body, which are rarely developed on their own but in concert with other bodies. Hunting gazelles obviously required coordination, skill, and equipment. But so too did the care of wild grasses, with their particular needs of water, sun, shade, and the scattering of seeds in order to reproduce.

People were engaged in a dance with other species and objects, where the requirements of other entities and those of humans formed joint rhythms and responses. Some reindeer herders today talk of 'reindeer magic', arising from the joined understandings of the herd and the herders. Power shifts between humans and herd as it does in all relationships, as the herders fully acknowledge. Their aim is not to dominate the animals, but to work with them to provide protection for the herd, but also food and transport for people. People are able to adjust to the rhythms of a number of species at once.

Farming was not an inevitable outcome of late Pleistocene experiments, but a gradual locking together of rhythms, which once they became more complex and interlinked suffered the dangers of dissonance and periodic collapse. The emphasis I have placed on working together might sketch a benign picture of people in harmony with nature. Harmonies are hard to achieve and impossible to sustain across the changing states of the world. Some respect for our partners across the planet allows us not just to negotiate new relationships, but to navigate their breakdown.

The last great global warming which shifted vegetation zones, the territories of animals, and sea levels was one of the most challenging periods in planetary history since the slow coming into being of *Homo sapiens*. Yet out of this long period came a mass of novel technologies, skills, and relationships which provided the basis for life after 11 kya when the world had warmed.

In our prehistories this has too often been seen as the time before farming, prior to the origins of complex modern societies. We are now starting to understand the deeper rhythmical processes of human life, the complexity of relationships involved, the lack of any linear directions, but also the legacies that the deeper past leaves behind. The Holocene consequences of Pleistocene relationships are the subject of the next chapter.

Chapter 5
Continental fusion— connections across Europe, Asia, and Africa

We think of globalization as a new process. It is true that the speed at which people and things can travel is novel, as is the potential for widely separated parts of the world to be connected. Movements and connections are part of all human history, although we have not always appreciated where centres of innovation and reception lie. One of the great realizations of recent years is that central Asia (composed of the Russian steppe and the various 'Stans' to the south) is not peripheral to the main action in China, India, Iran, Iraq, Europe, and the Mediterranean. Rather it is both a source of innovation and a mode of connecting the continent that has been so far unrecognized.

The idea of a Silk Road is a seductive one, but may not exist as a defined routeway in any period, certainly not before the last 2,000 years. More piecemeal, but effective, links may well have existed for many millennia and the crucial development was the domestication of the horse some 6 kya on the Russian steppe, south of the Urals. It is easier to form links across the same latitude due to similarities in vegetation, temperature, day length, and seasonality than it is north–south across the grain of a landmass. The steppe regions from the Ukraine to northern China have more similarities with each other ecologically and topographically than they do to the forested regions to the north or the deserts to their south. This promoted travel, contact, and the movement of plants, animals, and trade products along the grain of the continent.

To the south, the Indian Ocean has connected southeast Asia, south Asia, and Africa for at least the last 5,000 years. This is best evidenced by the movements of plants and animals, as we will see later. By later antiquity, trade is obvious between India, Rome to the west, and China to the east, but this is predicated on much older links and connections.

A seeming paradox of later prehistory is the creation of a great mosaic of local ways of life across Eurasia and Africa through selective dipping into the streams of movement in living things and materials over long distances. Here long-lasting attitudes to food, commensality, and ritual life, perhaps going back to the Pleistocene (see Chapter 4), structure patterns of what is accepted or rejected out of the flows across the planet. Local ways of life came about through connection, not isolation, with movements by both land and sea. Understanding both the flows and the forms that life has taken is a major contemporary research challenge. Globalization is new in the speed at which communication and travel is possible. Long-distance connections, however, are basic to being human.

A sketch of regional prehistories

Africa. Africa's later prehistory shows a series of dynamisms that are impossible to fit within a conventional notion of social evolution. For a start the division between hunter-gatherer and farmer is unhelpful, with people in many areas combining wild and domesticated plants and animals in complex and varied landscapes across the continent. Social arrangements cannot easily be lined up in a progression from simple to complex, from band to tribe, chiefdom to state. Instead, African social relations over the recent period exhibit a mix of lineage and clan-based forms, combined with those of age sets or modes of charismatic leadership less rooted in kinship.

It is likely that such variety existed in the past. State forms and cities grew up but without the modes of hierarchy we expect elsewhere in the world. Metallurgy did not follow the sequence of copper to bronze to iron found in Eurasia, with instead a much greater emphasis on iron south of the Sahara, with smaller pockets of bronze working in many cases later than iron working.

The earliest pottery in the world, outside of east Asia, developed in north Africa among hunter-gatherers before spreading to the Levant. The aesthetic systems of the continent are varied and extraordinary, from the textiles and pottery of west Africa, the metalwork of central Africa, and rock art in the south. The object world carried a complex of values concerning human biographies, links with the divine, and connections with other times and places.

We have a strong sense of current African biogeography—the largest desert in the world is the Sahara, with smaller deserts in the southwest and the Horn of Africa, which are counterbalanced by the tropical rainforests in west and central Africa, with dry savannah and grassland over large areas of east and south Africa. Climate change was out of phase with the north of the Mediterranean coming out of the last glacial, but had dramatic effects. Deep deserts in the Sahara today were once wooded grassland in the early Holocene, with huge lakes like so-called Lake MegaChad (at least fifty times the size of Lake Chad today), providing habitats for hippos, fish, crocodiles, and water for many grazing animals. Fluctuations between wet and dry have occurred in the Sahara throughout the Pleistocene, and wet phases may have aided hominins in finding routes out of Africa in the deep past. The state of the Sahara today is due to climate, but also overgrazing and deforestation on both its northern and southern borders.

Africa, past and present, has seen an enormous variety of landscape formations due to topographic variation, and the combinations of animals (mainly introduced) and plants (both from the outside and local) with a variety of material means and skills. None of the

fifty grazing animals native to Africa have been domesticated
(it was for a while thought that north or west Africa was a centre
of cattle domestication, but this is now discounted by most), so
that the major domesticates—sheep, goats, cows, pigs, dogs, and
chickens were introduced.

It is possible that donkeys in Africa derive in part from wild
populations in Nubia and/or Somalia and the guinea fowl is a
clear African domesticate in the first millennium AD in Sahel, with
a later complex genetic interchange with chickens. A glimpse at
the history of cattle gives us some sense of the tangled histories
around animals. The earliest dates for domesticated cattle are
around 9 kya on the grassy hinterlands of the Nile. They then
dispersed west and south. Zebu cattle came in from south Asia,
possibly only 1 kya. The earliest dates for cattle receive some
confirmation in human genetics as it is estimated that the mutation
needed to give people the ability to consume milk and break down
lactose occurred between 7 and 6 kya, showing that the close
relationship with another species has changed the human genome.

The genetics of cattle have altered within Africa to make some
breeds more resistant to blood parasites borne by the tsetse fly,
with west African breeds famously able to survive in tsetse-infected
regions. Some zebu-derived breeds resist ticks or heat, surviving
too with less water than others. Tsetse fly is most prevalent in
bushy habitats, so that people have both altered habitats through
burning, but also avoid such areas. We can see here a complex
and ever-changing relationship between cows, people, insects,
diseases, habitats, and the technologies of cattle keeping, with
human intentions just part of the mix of variables, which will
also have altered through shifts in climate and vegetation.

Complexity surrounding plants is similar in degree, although the
factors involved are different. Some plants, for instance pearl millet,
are native to west Africa, were domesticated over 2,400 years ago,
and several centuries later had reached India. Local domestication

is also seen for a range of plants, including ground nuts, T'ef, finger millet, varieties of yams, African rice, beans, and so on. Many were then adopted by people in southwest and south Asia, either in a wild or domesticated form. Other crops were introduced, which include the Middle Eastern cereals, most of which came via Egypt and Nubia, but also broomcorn and foxtail millets (both domesticated in northern China) and Asian rice from southern China.

Crops from southeast Asia and Papua New Guinea moved across the Indian Ocean in the last 2,000 years and maybe earlier, including taro and yams, bananas and sugar cane. The Indian Ocean has been vital for two-way interchanges, showing that over the last two millennia or more ocean travel across these distances has been common. African crops, both local and introduced, are propagated vegetatively and by seed, requiring varied management techniques, yearly cycles, and soil preparation. When the demands of animals are added to those of plants, a very complex mix of factors, skills, and modes of material culture ensue, which underlie the variety and dynamism of African landscape use and food cultures.

An important topic is the history of urbanism in Africa. Africa's ancient towns vary, but few of them meet the standard model as developed for the Middle East and Europe. Researchers such as Bassey Andah have attempted to come up with a checklist of traits more appropriate to African urbanism, emphasizing, among other elements, the tension between ritual and more secular forms of power. Towns are known over the last four millennia or more in places like Chad and Mali, the states of Benin and the Yoruba in west Africa, the Ethiopian highlands, and the Great Lakes region. There is a tension between long-distance exchange and local modes of power, with the latter building more on lateral connections than social hierarchy.

One of the most discussed urban centres is that of Great Zimbabwe, which is itself one of a number of polities found between the Zambezi River to the north and the Limpopo to the south from the early first millennium to the middle second millennium AD. These were based variously on agriculture around sorghum, millet, beans, and cowpeas, with cattle often an important source of wealth.

There was considerable exchange into Indian Ocean links, which had been active for millennia, as we have seen. The African polities exported gold and ivory for Persian and Far Eastern stoneware and porcelain, Indian glass beads, and cloth. Great Zimbabwe itself was constructed of walled enclosures, including the so-called Great Enclosure, with evidence of the residences of commoners and artisans around these. At its peak during the 14th and 15th centuries Great Zimbabwe may have had a population of 20,000 people.

Older interpretations saw the polity animated by tensions between ritual and secular specialists. More recent work by Innocent Pikirayi and Shadreck Chirikure have emphasized the dynamic nature of the polity, with the various enclosures best seen as shifting centres of power, but also emphasizing the levels of craft production in the settlement and the production of inequality over its history. The control of water in a semi-arid landscape is also emerging as crucial. As with urban sites everywhere, African towns pose problems to fieldworkers because of their size and internal complexity. But it is also necessary to produce African-based models more suitable to the developments of politics and trade, and contrasting with the perceived path of social evolution elsewhere.

Europe and Asia. We have already seen something of the movement of plants and animals across Europe and Asia, deriving in part from the experiments of the late glacial. In the west, the so-called Mesolithic peoples of Europe were spread everywhere from the Mediterranean to the Arctic, creating ways of life out of local plants, animals, and materials, which had interwoven histories lasting the first 5,000 years or more of the Holocene. People had spread onto Mediterranean islands maybe well back into the Pleistocene, but places like Cyprus were occupied from the Levant over 10 kya, as were Aegean islands.

By the mid-Holocene many islands were inhabited, which often involved replacement of native plants and animals by introduced ones, with places like Cyprus seeing regular introductions of goats, pigs, and cattle (not an easy animal to transport on a boat) starting at least 10 kya. Domesticated plants and animals, presumably with human colonists, moved overland from Anatolia 8.5 kya reaching central Europe a millennium later and the Atlantic seaboard five centuries after that.

In southeast Europe, villages of mudbrick houses turned into tells, rising above the plains of the Danube, and were occupied in copper-using times before being abandoned on a wide scale some 5.9 kya. Why this widespread abandonment occurred is debated, with possible climate and cultural breakdown both being canvassed. From the Hungarian Plains to the Atlantic coast in France and the Low Countries a new form of Neolithic is found, with wooden long houses probably accommodating both people and animals, with pots with linear decorations after the which the Linearbandkeramik culture is named.

To the east, in Romania and the Ukraine, an extraordinary phenomenon is seen in the Cucuteni-Trypillia group, where, for two centuries from 5.6 kya, the largest sites in Europe were created, at least as large as early Uruk, with five sites ranging in size from 220 hectares (Nebelivka) to 450 or 340 hectares at Talianky (Figure 7). At Maydanetskoe, 1,575 structures have been documented in an area of 181 hectares and, at Talianky, nearly 1,400 structures were recognized through geophysical prospection in an area of 232 hectares. The largest sites may have had 8,000–10,000 people in them. Whether these can be called towns is a matter of considerable debate, but the population levels were

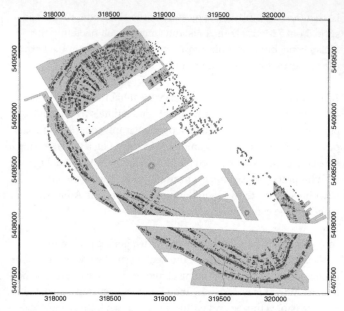

7. The mega-site at Talianky—hundreds of houses are organized
concentrically.

beyond the limits of a face-to-face community where everyone
could easily interact and communicate, indicating perhaps that
these were combinations of smaller settlements which came to
cluster around a dominant group.

There is no real evidence of social hierarchy, and although some
larger buildings are now apparent these might well be communal
rather than the dwellings of the powerful. These mega-sites are
a mystery, partly because they do not fit any evolutionary or
developmental model. There are no earlier large settlements,
and subsequently we found small dispersed hamlets. The next
settlements of a similar size in this area were medieval.

On the western fringes of Europe, in places like the British Isles,
settlements are generally hard to find in the Neolithic and early

Bronze Age periods, probably because there was considerable mobility, despite the domesticated plants and animals that had been introduced to Britain around 6.2 kya (probably having accompanied human colonists).

The Neolithic stone-built village of Skara Brae in Orkney, revealed by a big storm in 1850, had houses with striking internal organization including stone beds and dressers. Occupied for 500 years from 5.2 kya, its inhabitants lived from the sea and small-scale farming. The village is part of one of the most impressive Neolithic landscapes in Europe, with the huge chambered tomb of Maeshowe and the stone circles such as the Ring of Brodgar and at Stenness.

Elsewhere in Britain, settlement evidence is rare, but the monuments, such as stone circles, causewayed camps, and henges (i.e. circular structures with an external bank, internal ditch, and four entrances) remain striking elements of the landscape today. Stonehenge (which started in the Neolithic and its stones erected in the early Bronze Age) is the most famous of these henges. Neolithic landscapes materialized cosmologies in which the movements of the sun and moon were important to orientations on the ground. The stones for Stonehenge were brought from the Preseli Mountains 250 kilometres (140 miles) away in south Wales, perhaps indicating that some special properties were perceived in these rocks. When the first field systems were laid out some 3.5 kya, they had alignments probably on the summer and winter solstice. These alignments carried on in field systems through to the end of the Roman period, after which a medieval landscape was laid out around AD 850 influenced by Christianity. In our own lives we make distinctions between the pragmatic, the religious, and the magical, but such distinctions did not always hold in the same way in earlier times.

The efficacy of Bronze Age farming depended on ploughing, sowing, and manuring all at the right times and on the correct soil and slope, but it was also underpinned by the fact that the fields were oriented towards the sun in key seasons and perhaps also because the human dead were buried nearby. A great variety of settlement, farming, and foraging existed across Neolithic and Bronze Age Europe always linked with more ritualized features of the landscape.

An important development from the Neolithic onwards is a monumentalizing of burial. Along the Atlantic seaboard from Scandinavia to Iberia, but also through France and in a couple of areas on the north Mediterranean coast, are found passage graves, with a central stone-built passage and chambers off. For at least 1,000 years, starting 6.5 kya, people buried the dead collectively. Often the dead were not interred as whole bodies, instead chambers full of arms, legs, skulls, and torsos are known. People were buried as members of the group, rather than as individuals. For groups regulated by kinship, genealogical connections provided rights to land, trade, and ritual as well as organizing marriages.

Earthen mounds with no inner chamber are also common along the Atlantic seaboard and it may be that these were modelled on Linearbandkeramik longhouses, which might make them houses of the dead. The similarities in burial practices along the Atlantic coast alert us to the mass of local and long-distant trade connections that existed from the Neolithic onwards, with stones, amber, and coral surviving to indicate trade between small groups, which probably originally included a mass of organic materials that have mainly perished.

Neolithic groups were likely to have been small in number and in the scale of the landscape use, but each was part of a dense network of cooperation and rivalry, where control of exchange relations was important to shifting patterns of social standing. Although these groups were small there is surprising evidence of violence on a regular basis, but also through dramatic instances such as Talheim. Here, around 7 kya, thirty-four individuals (sixteen children, eighteen adults) were buried in a pit with a combination of injuries from stone axes and arrows.

The nature of the injuries indicate they may have been fleeing when killed; some had earlier, healed injuries from previous violent episodes. The age composition of the group demonstrates that this was a whole community who were killed, with some other broadly contemporary 'massacre' sites found in Neolithic Europe. Trade and massacre might seem to be at opposite ends of the social scale, but were all part of rivalries and alliances that may well have had a volatile nature among small Neolithic groups organized in many different ways across Europe.

Materials create connections, so that stone and pottery shaped ancient networks, but metallurgy has formed a vital medium of interaction over the last few millennia, not least because it can be melted down and recycled. Pottery, supposedly a crucial feature of the Neolithic revolution, started in the Palaeolithic; metallurgy, the prime definition of the metal ages (the Copper, Bronze, and Iron Ages), first occurred in the Neolithic, indeed before full farming had commenced, its use starting in Anatolia in the tenth millennium BC.

The older history of metallurgy emphasized function, with the provision of better cutting edges and finer, more durable tools. The long history of metals now apparently shows that for many thousands of years, people were attracted by colour and malleability. Copper minerals (e.g. malachite, azurite) were used for personal ornamentation (and occasionally as part of burial rituals), perhaps for several millennia. Brightly coloured minerals would have led people to search for ore deposits in the mountains, leading also to the discovery of occasional rare finds of native copper, and ultimately to the smelting of the ores, perhaps initially as the result of some accidental heating of malachite. Smelted copper started in Eurasia in Anatolia, perhaps in the ninth millennium BC, before spreading to southeast Europe and the Middle East by the seventh millennium BC. The technology of copper smelting subsequently spread to all of Eurasia by the fourth millennium BC.

An independent origin is presumed for the smelting of copper in the New World, and has also been suggested for parts of Eurasia, particularly China, although most would now see an introduction of bronze metallurgy into China from the steppe as having been around 4 kya. Bronze metallurgy was very rare in Africa and its origins still debated, although local development is entirely possible. Copper and then bronze (an alloy of copper with tin or lead) have a complex inter-relationship with gold and silver and all these metals can be melted and remelted. There is currently a shift in thinking about bronze, moving away from using chemical analyses to link artefacts to ore bodies in an attempt to understand trade towards an acceptance that recycling was always common. New techniques focus on the loss of minor minerals through repeated melting and casting, allowing researchers to track streams of bronze across Eurasia.

Metals were mined, smelted, and cast, involving a great range of tools, techniques, and materials (such as charcoal, wax, and clay, each of which has its own connections), many of which concern percussion through mining and fine control of fire when smelting and casting. Skill is needed and dangers abound, so it no surprise that in many more recent societies metal workers are seen to have the magical powers required to control the strong forces of destruction and creation.

Iron has different history to bronze. Its sources are more ubiquitous but its working tricky, so that high temperatures are needed, as well as techniques such as quenching, where the metal is taken from a red-hot state to cold through immersing in liquid. The Chinese developed abilities to generate high temperatures through refined pottery production (porcelain was produced over 4 kya, requiring temperatures of around 1,400 degrees Celsius to vitrify the clay). Iron was cast in China around 2,500 years ago, which was not possible for Europeans until the early modern period. The first iron working, probably using meteoric iron, started in western Eurasia at least 5 kya , but iron was not smelted for another 1,000 years.

Materials connected Eurasia in ways that we are just starting to understand. Our ability to map the movement of materials will soon be linked to genetic results on the movements of people, plants, and animals, allowing a much fuller picture of human and material movements.

The Bronze Age was defined by its eponymous metal, which was seen in older views as being technologically superior. As is so often seen, efficiency of function does not seem to have been a paramount consideration to people of the ancient world, with the variety of form and colour of bronze artefacts exciting attention, as well as the need to trade with other groups for the components of bronze. Increasingly, indications exist of Eurasian connections from the late Neolithic into the Bronze Age.

Horses were first ridden and probably domesticated around 6 kya, opening up the vast grassland steppes in a way that was impossible to people travelling on foot, given the dispersed nature of food edible for humans in grasslands. The first wheeled vehicles were probably invented around 6 kya and these were pulled by cattle. Wagons allowed materials to be transported, assisting mobile lifestyles in which the materials (houses, hunting, foraging, and cooking equipment, food, rich items for exchange, very small children) could be moved, albeit only a few miles every day.

These people lived mainly on animal products, eating plants such as wild goose foot (Chenopodium) in small amounts. By 5 kya groups using late Neolithic Corded Ware pottery are found from the Urals to the eastern French border. Recent genetic work indicates flows of people from east to west, although some of the claims for mass migration need further substantiation. A few hundred years later bronze was in use, with Corded Ware groups connecting with so-called Yamnaya groups further east.

The late Neolithic and early Bronze Age periods on the steppe, from eastern Siberia to western Europe, were clearly periods of considerable change, but little archaeological work has been carried out over huge areas and we are confronted by a mass of groups with confusing names. There has also been a tendency to link these groups and their movements to the expansion of Indo-European speakers. This is a temptation I have resisted as direct evidence linking language, settlements, and artefacts is lacking, but we need to consider the issues.

The prehistory of language

In 1796, Sir William Jones, chief justice of India and founder of the Royal Asiatic Society, presented a famous discourse on Indian culture in which he pointed out the similarities between the ancient language of India, Sanskrit, and numerous other languages, such as Persian, Greek, Latin, and the Germanic and Celtic languages, found across Europe and Asia.

The word for fire, for instance, is *agnis* in Sanskrit and *ignis* in Latin, from which English takes the word 'ignite'. All the languages of Europe (with a few exceptions, such as Basque, Hungarian, Estonian, and Finnish), some Asian languages, such as Armenian and Persian, and a large number of Indian languages, have been grouped together and termed 'Indo-European' languages. Jones sought an origin for these languages in the diaspora thought to have happened after Noah's ark had landed, which is not an origin many would accept today. However, a great deal of effort has gone into reconstructing proto-Indo-European on the basis of similarities in the forms of words known today and systematic changes in their form over time. The surprising, but undeniable, basis of historical linguistics is the fact that there are systematic sound changes between one language and another, for instance *ph* in Greek regularly becomes *b* in Germanic languages—thus the Greek *phrater*, 'clan member', becomes English *brother*. Systematic changes allow connections to be made and histories to be reconstructed.

In the 1980s, almost 200 years after William Jones, Colin Renfrew became interested in whether the origins of the Indo-Europeans could be linked to changes in the archaeological evidence. Indeed, Renfrew looked forward to a 'grand synthesis' of archaeology, historical linguistics, and genetics. In considering the distribution of Indo-European languages he felt that there was only one episode or process over the last few thousand years that could be responsible for such a widespread distribution of related languages, and that was the spread of farming and farmers. He and others subsequently broadened the farming-origins hypothesis to account for the origins and spread of other broadly distributed language groups. Chief among these was the Niger–Congo group of western, central, and southern Africa, which was thought to have been carried from west Africa by the migration of Bantu agriculturalists; and the Austronesian languages found throughout southeast Asia (with an outlier in Madagascar), the coastal languages of Papua New Guinea and the Solomons, and out into the Pacific as far as Hawai'i, Easter Island, and New Zealand, which was thought to have been spread by farmers originally from Taiwan.

Languages might have spread through connections, rather than human population movements. Is it also possible that the distribution of Indo-European languages first occurred in the late Palaeolithic when there are widespread similarities in material culture across wide areas of Eurasia, to be reinforced and reordered by later contacts. This proposal does not conflict with archaeological evidence, but it is hard to test against current evidence of ancient DNA and finds little support among linguists (partly because anything occurring so long ago is beyond the range of historical reconstruction). But it must be said that no proposal so far has pleased a majority in all three disciplines. Similarly, in the Austronesian area, indications from genetics do not show evidence of a homeland in Taiwan, the proximate origin of farming groups, but in eastern Indonesia, where there is no particular evidence of origins of farming.

The links between language, genetics, and archaeology look anything but clear-cut and the hypothesis of farming spreads is not bearing up well, even in Africa where the Bantu migrations are not accepted by some archaeologists, and the genetic evidence is not well understood, but obviously very complicated.

The Australian languages are not related to any outside the continent (the only possible exception being those of the highlands of New Guinea), indicating some ancient divergence between them and all other language families. The languages of the Americas are still surprisingly controversial. Na-Dene languages of North America form a tight group, presumably due to recent origins, but many of the languages of the rest of the continent are lumped, rather than grouped in any typological sense, and their unity is very dubious.

Returning to Eurasian connections, we see that in the western Caucasus Mountains on the northeastern shore of the Black Sea, the so-called Maikop Bronze Age group came into being around 5.8 kya. In 1897, Russian archaeologist Nikolai Veselovskii excavated a huge tumulus near the town of Maikop. The tumulus was 10 metres high and 200 metres in diameter, covering a timber-built grave chamber divided into three sections in which were buried a man and two women. The male burial contained turquoise and carnelian beads, bronze weapons and cauldrons, stone tools, silver drinking vessels with animal decoration, gold animal appliqués presumably originally sewn onto a tunic, and six silver rods with gold and silver bull figurine terminals. The Maikop tumulus is the most spectacular of 150–250 rich burials in the north Caucasus. Early discussions of this material saw influences from Mesopotamia far to the south. Despite some southern stylistic links, most now see the Maikop burials and settlements as being of local derivation.

Art

Decorated pottery and metalwork from Maikop prompt discussion of a topic we have not broached so far: that of art. Art is a tricky term, as it has many present-day implications, making us think of paintings, sculpture, and fine objects in museums and galleries across the world. Over the long duration of human history finely crafted and decorated items were probably part of the flow of life, albeit a special part. In Europe the earliest items we designate as art were found at least 30 kya in the form of paintings on cave walls during the Ice Age in France, Spain, and elsewhere together with carvings in bone and ivory of people and animals, and some clay models.

Art of Greece and Rome, together with that from the Renaissance onwards in Europe, has been lauded as being true to life and realistic. By contrast, most so-called 'primitive' art was thought to be by artists incapable of realism. Some of the most stunningly realistic images and statuary dates from the Ice Age, from hunter-gatherers working by torchlight in areas of caves difficult to access. Working in either three or two dimensions people created images of horses, lions, and humans worthy of Stubbs or Degas. An evolutionary history of art, in which people gradually improved their work through better materials, techniques, and application, is impossible to sustain. We should look instead at why people created images and objects, and whether so-called realism was desired or not in the roles they played. Much emphasis has been placed on the magico-religious dimension to art, wondering whether animals were depicted or carved to give people some power over them or to express a form of kinship.

At the end of August 1939 the excavations of the Stadel Cave on the Hohlenstein in Germany were brought to an end by the imminence of war and, among other things, numerous fragments of mammoth ivory were packed up. It was not until 1989 that the fragments were fully fitted together, revealing a 30-centimetre-high statue, with the head of a lion and body of a male human (Figure 8). The limbs have a leonine character, as has the head. Horizontal grooves on the upper arm indicate tattoos or scarification. More recent excavations at Stadel Cave indicate that the statue might be 40,000 years old. This statue was not just a reproduction of reality, but a play with it, especially of the boundaries between people and other species. A third animal is involved, as the statue was made from the tusk of a young mammoth, hard to work from the tough dentine. The amount of effort (it is calculated that the statue would have needed at least 400 hours to produce) suggests

8. **The Lion Man from Stadel Cave.**

that the maker and users of the statue were wrestling with important issues of culture and philosophy, in which the links to other powerful species were at stake.

Rock art continues through the Neolithic and Bronze Ages, with northern latitudes of Eurasia seeing a continuous band of rock art sites, well studied in places like Scandinavia, but distributed across to the eastern seaboard of Siberia. To us rock looks like a surface onto which images are painted, pecked, or engraved. But it could have been seen as the boundary between two worlds, with the images on the rock surface appearing from another dimension. We cannot know earlier mindsets for sure, but ancient imagery alerts us to the sheer difference of their practices.

Areas within present-day China see a precocious emphasis on fine materials, with jade carved regularly from the Neolithic with some extraordinarily fine pottery, such as the egg-shell-thin black wares of the Longshan group. The development of copper, gold, and silver working adds a new dimension to human artefacts. Metalwork from the large Maikop tumulus in the form of animals is regularly seen as the origin of later Scythian or Sarmatian styles on the steppe in the last millennium BC. Origins are difficult to judge, but there is a considerable emphasis on animals such as horses, birds, occasional predators, and hybrids, such as gryphons, in both earlier and later metalwork.

Both Celtic and Scythian art play with dimensions (what often appears to be two animals on a piece of metalwork might just be one of which we can see both the left and right sides at once) and transformations (there are many hybrids in ancient art—gryphons, sphinxes, as well as people turning into animals or vegetation). The motifs of Scythian and Celtic art might differ in detail, but right across Eurasia in the first millennium BC a similar sensibility was in play. This might be called 'animistic', where objects we think are inert (such as metalwork, stones in a landscape, etc.)

could be considered to have active properties, and the boundaries between the living and non-living are fluid.

Art is not a passive reflection of the world, but a means of shaping thought and action in it. Statues, carvings, and paintings might be better seen as experiments rather than representations, as people tried to understand how the world worked and how they could work in the world. As the lion-person from Stadel shows, such experiments have lasted at least 40,000 years and continue to this day.

Metalwork came to be organized on a considerable scale with evidence of mining and large settlements home to many craft workers, such as that of Sintashta east of the Urals. The Sintashta settlement was 140 metres in diameter with a timber-reinforced earthen wall with originally probably fifty to sixty houses, each of which had ovens, hearths, slag, and copper, just over 4 kya. Even more striking was the fact that in burials under mounds were the oldest chariots in the world. Chariots have spoked wheels, unlike the solid wooden wheels on carts, with light frames and bodies. Construction of chariots required considerable carpentry skills, especially to make light, but strong, spoked wheels, metal fittings, and leatherwork; to drive a chariot at speed over rough ground hones skills of horsemanship and, if they are used for hunting or war, the ability to throw a spear or fire an arrow from a moving vehicle must be developed.

Sintashta is a centre of innovation, the effects of which stretch from the Urals to the central plains of China. We left China in the previous chapter with a story of the domestication of rice, millets, and probably some vegetable crops. China also developed the world's first pottery. Furthermore, we saw that plants came from tropical southeast Asia and Papua New Guinea, as well as important inputs from the west, such as wheat, barley, sheep, and cattle. Out of these various inputs Chinese groups created integrated systems for plants and animals by about 7 kya. Again terminology is confusing, as full farming is only first found in the so-called middle Neolithic along the Yellow and Yangtze rivers and on the Luan and Liao rivers flowing into Bohai Bay northeast of Beijing. Now carved jades are found in numbers, as well as decorated pottery used for ritual drinking of wine. Large ceremonial centres occur in the middle Neolithic with big public buildings and evidence of complex production of pottery, jade, and stone. Some richer burials are found, perhaps indicating growing social inequality. The late Neolithic (5–4 kya) saw accelerating change with large sites of the Longshan group along the middle Yellow Valley and elsewhere that had large populations, often enclosed by massive rammed-earth walls and ditches, with temple complexes and industrial areas. Longshan pottery is incredibly fine walled and now variegates into a great range of shapes for the serving and drinking of rice wine. When bronze appears after 4 kya these same pottery forms are cast in metal. Rudimentary script appears on pottery and jade objects ancestral to later writing. At sites such as Taosi small copper bells and bronze objects occur alongside very elaborate jade and polychrome ceramics.

Bronze metallurgy enters China from the central Asian steppes, with groups like Sintashta providing an initial impetus, and contacts maintained through later Bronze Age Andronovo and Karasuk cultures through Khazakhstan and the Altai and Sayan Mountains which border present-day Xinjiang, the westernmost extension of China. Chariots, originating in Sintashta, east of the Urals, rapidly moved south into the urban lands of Mesopotamia, Egypt, and the eastern Mediterranean, but also east to China. The idea that the major civilizations were the origins of all important developments is doubtful, as an apparently peripheral group proves to be a centre of innovation and influence. Soon after adopting bronze, the Chinese were able to produce a staggering complexity and range of forms (mainly in ritual vessels) using piece-mould casting unprecedented anywhere else in the world. Such precocious developments in metal were enabled by a long history of ceramics requiring high and controlled temperatures.

Our story in China comes to an end with the early states of Erlitou and Erligang (3.9–3.25 kya) which develop writing to create a dynastic history. The central plains of China saw some of the largest and densest populations in the world from the middle Neolithic onwards, drawing to them outside innovations. New plants, animals, and materials, arriving over centuries, helped create the conditions whereby large populations were subjected to inequalities, and new modes of religion and ritual took over; the states of Shang and Zhou were the result.

We have come to divide up Europe, the steppe, and eastern Asia into regions with their own histories and trajectories. With the opening up of the former Soviet Union and China it is now possible to see the depth and importance of connections across this huge region from the Neolithic onwards. Materials, such as bronze, and complex art styles linked to shared cosmologies and practices, helped set up and maintain connections that all areas participated in and benefitted from.

Connections did not produce similarities of culture, however, and regional differences increase from the Bronze Age onwards. At the eastern and western ends of Eurasia groups embrace farming and increasingly sedentary lifestyles; on the steppe people learn how to be mobile, organizing their lives over huge areas and through the various temporal phases of the community made up of humans, plants, and animals. Archaeology has concentrated on the development of sedentism, but we need to think more about how mobility was organized and sustained. It is likely that sedentism is only really possible in concert with movement, so that the emerging cities of the south and the so-called nomads of the north brought each other into being.

Chapter 6
New worlds—the Americas, Australia, and the Pacific

For many, the world is full of energies to be understood, worked with, and placated. Westerners are inclined to call such energies 'spiritual' or 'cosmological', but spirits appear to us now a bit like fairies, something only the credulous believe in. However, for those who do believe, these are forces of creation and destruction, which permeate everything in the same way as do the processes of physics, chemistry, and biology for us. People felt themselves related to spiritual forces. Much of life across the globe, including the areas I will look at here—the Americas, Australia, and the Pacific—were organized around understanding and living with the spirits of the earth and the heavens.

Cosmological relations form the thread I shall follow through the complex forms of evidence from these continents, which cover a large part of the earth's surface and of global prehistory. Many groups in these areas have been labelled 'hunter-gatherers', a very inadequate term for the variety of engagements people had with wild plants and animals, combined also with domesticated forms on occasion. The constraining aspect of the notion of hunter-gatherer will be a further theme.

The Americas

In Chapter 3, we saw that our modern human ancestors arose in Africa some 300 kya, leaving that continent at least 90 kya, and spreading through Europe and Asia by 40 kya. There has been more controversy over the early human history of the Americas than any other continent. There have been claims of occupation 80 kya or more, but these are not really controversial, because they lack an empirical basis. Given that people entered the Americas from Siberia it is surprising that there are two sites in South America, Pedra Furada in Brazil and Monte Verde in Chile, which may be older than any found in North America, possibly first used by people 30 kya. Monte Verde, in south-central Chile, has an undoubted occupation in an open-air site 13 kya, with evidence preserved in a peat bog of log foundations for huts, a piece of mastodon flesh, a human footprint, animal skins, plant remains, and wooden and stone tools (Figure 9).

This sedentary occupation undermines the notion that early inhabitants were mobile hunter-gatherers, and the site shows trade

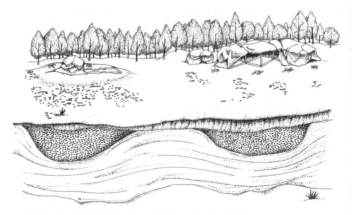

9. **Reconstruction of the site at Monte Verde, Chile.**

links with other groups. But the possibility that there might be an occupation some 20,000 years older is controversial and troubling, and one that Tom Dillehay, the excavator of the site, seems increasingly doubtful about. Below the main layers are a possible hearth and possible tools dating to 30 kya, the qualifications receiving greater emphasis as time goes by. Pedra Furada in eastern Brazil has produced dates between 32 and 17 kya. There is considerable scepticism (especially among North American archaeologists) about these dates, as the charcoal may come from natural fires and the stone tools could have been created when stones on the top of the cliff above the site washed down, suffering natural fractures mimicking those produced by people.

The earliest accepted settlement is associated with the so-called Clovis culture. In 1932 large blade tools were found near the town of Clovis, New Mexico, in association with the bones of extinct animals. Clovis points have now been found in every state of the Union, up into the Arctic Circle, and deep into South America. Radiocarbon dates place these sites at 12 kya, with another horizon of Folsom points about 2,000 years later.

Clovis represents the first undoubted occupation of a continent inhabited by so-called megafauna, such as mammoths, sabre-toothed tigers, giant moose, and a species of beaver the size of a modern bear, making the continent very attractive to hunters. It seems most likely that people walked from present-day Siberia, which was inhabited from at least 23 kya, with distributions of leaf-shaped points covering northeastern Siberia, Alaska, and western Canada by 15 kya. Glaciations producing periods of lower sea level have created a land bridge across the Bering Sea (so-called Beringia) at least four times in the last 60,000 years and this has led to migrations of a range of animal species from Asia to America.

Humans may have been deterred by the relative paucity of game in Beringia itself, a somewhat barren area, and the size of the ice-sheets across Alaska. Alternatively they may have gone down the coast, travelling by sea, as did the first entrants into Australia, which would make some sense of early dates in somewhere like Monte Verde. I would be happy with early dates from South America, but accept that the present evidence is not overwhelming. On the basis of the distributions of leaf-shaped points down into eastern Canada and the fact that the 13,000-year-old occupation at Monte Verde does not look like the initial stages of colonization, I would opt for an initial date of some 15 kya for the first colonization of the Americas, leaving time for the build-up of population which led to the widespread visibility of Clovis sites some 3,000 years later.

America has a complex series of ecological zones from the arctic and taiga regions of northern Canada, to the large areas of woodland down the east and west of North America, with the grassland plains in between. Deserts are found in the southwest and Great Basin of the US, but also on the coastal zone of Chile. Rainforests have a northern extension in Florida, but are found throughout central America and the vast Amazon Basin, with grasslands and temperate forest again further south. The enormous mosaic of habitats is influenced by temperature, rainfall, and altitude, but has also been continuously altered by people over at least 15 kya. The earliest evidence for how people lived, from the Clovis, Folsom, and so-called Archaic periods emphasizes hunting, with less evidence of plant foods.

Plants became more important as the Holocene unfolded, with a huge series of experiments, including the use of root crops in the Southwest, Eastern Woodlands, and Great Plains, but also small seeds, succulent fruits and berries, nuts, and greens. In areas like the Great Basin, California, and the northwest agriculture was not practiced before historic times, with seeds, roots, and berries used at different times of the year; acorns and pine nuts were processed and stored; wild grasses were extensively gathered. Shifts in plant processing and cooking can be seen, with a prevalence of grinders before 3000 BC in California and more clay balls to aid boiling afterwards, perhaps indicating a shift towards acorns and away from grasses.

The earliest forms of domestication in South America took place on the coast prior to 10 kya, involving staples like gourds, potato, and manioc, but also tasty foods including avocados, chilli peppers, and beans. These were introduced into inland Andean sites from 6.2 kya onwards, with the tasty foods moving as early as the staples and each valley choosing its own roster of crops. Food is vital for defining identity in the present and so too in the past, with each valley group making small but significant variations in their diet which marked them out as different. Mexico also constituted a centre of plant experiment, with foods such as beans, squashes, and maize eventually emerging as crucial. Some plants were long used, but not domesticated, such as the seeds of the grass Setaria, which is biologically related to the millets of China that were domesticated.

One of the most amazing instances of the global story of domestication was the transformation of teosinte, with a cob the size of a little finger containing hard and difficult-to-detach grains, into maize which is now one of the most important of all global crops. Domestication started some 9 kya , probably in southern Mexico, with cultivation beginning some 2,000 years later. Village life did not coalesce until around 3,500 years later in places like Mexico, so that much of this plant experiment was by people who were semi-mobile.

Maize was introduced into the American southwest some 3.6 kya, initially into a diet based on a great range of grasses, nuts, and greens. By 2.4 kya isotopic studies of human bone show maize was the major element of diet, joined now by beans and squashes, and contributing to a much more settled lifestyle. In the Eastern Woodlands maize is first found from 2.3 kya but was incorporated into indigenous crop husbandry with small-seeded grasses, native squash, and sunflower. It is only from 1,200 years ago onwards that maize became the dominant crop, underwriting some of the most striking developments in prehistoric North America. Maize gradually spread up the eastern seaboard, providing the basis, in the last thousand years or so, for sedentary villages in many areas.

Much of human life throughout the Americas was mobile in different ways, but from around 3 kya large centres of population become evident in places like lowland Mexico, the American southwest, and the Mississippian region. Around 3.2 kya, both along the Mississippi and in the region of Mexico inhabited by the Olmec, large and carefully structured sites are found. The most impressive early example of such a site in North America is called Poverty Point in the lower Mississippi valley, although mound building itself goes back over 6,000 years. The core of Poverty Point was composed of an area of roughly 200 hectares, dominated by six concentric constructed ridges with houses on them, as well as five mounds (Figure 10). People lived on fish, deer, and nuts among other things.

Mound building is found in the preceding Middle Archaic, some 5.8–4.6 kya, with a hiatus in evidence until 3.6 kya when Poverty Point starts. Mound B and the ridges on which houses were built were constructed 3.4 kya and then Mound A was erected in a swamp, not an easy feat in itself, but combining also an interest in earth and water. There was a careful choice of sediments used to build the mound, which might help materialize myths of origin.

Another striking feature of the site is the massive amount of stone for making tools, all brought into the Mississippi valley which lacked stone sources. Some stone came from 500 kilometres and much from 1,000 kilometres away, worked into both utilitarian and non-utilitarian items. The amount of stone being moved was in excess of any functional need and we might think of pilgrimage, in which people travel to sacred places and the materials they

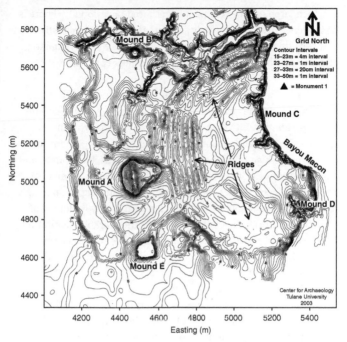

10. **Poverty Point, Mississippi Valley, showing the ridges on which houses were built and Mounds A–E.**

bring back connect them to those places. Long-distance exchanges are found prior to Poverty Point (although there is some hiatus of connections immediately before its construction), showing the long historical importance of such links. The massive effort in making complex cult centres to allow play with cosmology is very striking.

None of this fits the normal view of hunter-gatherers, constrained by subsistence. Many questions remain about Poverty Point, not least whether it was a centre with a large long-term population (something like a hunter-gatherer town, in other words) or whether it had a smaller permanent population who looked after a centre at which large numbers of people gathered occasionally. There is no evidence of social hierarchy, despite the size of the constructions and coordination of labour needed. These were self-organizing groups, mobilized by important cosmological concerns.

At a similar time, just over 3 kya (probably coincidentally), people constructed complex features in the Olmec region of Mexico—the fluted pyramid at La Venta may echo local eroded volcanoes and the plaza running from the pyramid has an alignment just off north. We also find large basalt carved heads, ball courts, and a possible script, with complex artistic iconography. Olmec villages were common, supported by agriculture based on maize, beans, and squash, themselves deriving from many millennia of experiment. While the Olmec provided considerable inspiration for the later Maya there is little indication of influence on Mississippian societies, which seem to have moved under their own historical impetuses.

Mesoamerican influence is more obvious on the US southwest (current national divisions are obviously not helpful here)—from 1,800 years ago large numbers of settlements are found here, but also impressive ritual structures, known as kivas. By 1,200 years ago some large sites were constructed, especially Chaco Canyon, reaching a peak 1 kya, with an incredibly complex mode of architecture, based on round structures.

The so-called Great Houses have been compared with palaces and they are quite different in organization and intent to later pueblos in the same area, even though both have a broadly religious purpose. Paquimé, a large complex that flourished between AD 1200 and 1450 in present-day Mexico, exhibited sophisticated symbolism combining land and water, with many canals between earthen mounds. Plumed serpents in the art show the influence of Mesoamerica, as do ball courts, but local peculiarities occur, including the ritual killing of 300 scarlet macaws, which were probably bred for sacrifice, along with bush turkeys. Religious ideas did not exist simply as ideas in people's heads, they were made real, bloody, and transformative through nurturing and killing as well as striking imagery.

Great effort has gone into investigating later Mississippian sites, not least the major centre at Cahokia in the so-called American Bottom near where the Missouri meets the Mississippi. Here the Monks Mound is the largest structure in ancient North America, only outdone in volume elsewhere in the world by the biggest Mayan and Egyptian pyramids or the First Emperor's tomb in China. At Cahokia astronomical alignments are very striking, as is a play on earth and water, because the site was constructed around a number of lakes.

Dramatic ceremony and sacrifice are evidenced through deposits of objects and people in the floors of abandoned houses, and in pits containing the bodies of young women, unlikely to have died together through natural causes. Cahokia was colonial, with similar sites found way to the north on the Mississippi and this network of sites traded. Cahokia itself was formed through a so-called 'big bang' around AD 1050, when the site suddenly expanded from around 1,000 to 10,000–15,000 inhabitants. Quite why this happened is unknown. Cahokia lasted at its peak for a century and in an other hundred years was abandoned entirely, to be forgotten. We assume hierarchical organization existed, with intense agriculture around the site, with fields of maize, squash, and beans and much produce stored to support a non-farming element of the population. Cahokia is a brief, dramatic, and mysterious episode, but its brief flourishing and decline is echoed elsewhere.

The northern part of the American continent from at least present-day Mexico to the Great Lakes has been criss-crossed by religious connections for the last 3,000 years or more. We can think in terms of pilgrimage and spiritual journeys taken by people and traversed by objects of which the imperishable elements only really survive. Occasionally over this long period extraordinary centres have crystallized out in the interstices of connections, with combinations of mounds, burials, water, and many people often carefully organized around celestial alignments (and therefore probably the change of the seasons).

Enormous amounts of physical effort went into sculpting the landscape, and in the absence of pack animals all the work was carried out by humans. Many of these communities were egalitarian and some were hunter-gatherers, so that work was undertaken through conviction and belief, not coercion, in many cases. Although sites like Cahokia have been long investigated, the staggering nature of individual sites has only recently been appreciated, as has the totality of the phenomena, where sites and connections differ over space and time, but definitely bear comparison one with another. The careful construction of mounds, using material selected from the local landscape, also makes me think of the kurgans of Eurasia, not that there is any connection, but in the sense that people are carefully and materially mapping their landscapes.

Native American society underwent a massive and traumatic transformation as white settlement advanced, with the horse and gun being introduced as features of life of great use to mobile hunters. By the time of the first European incursions in the 16th century sites like Cahokia were long forgotten, so that they feature little, if at all, in current native histories. In these large religious sites we are looking at extraordinary phenomena which were sufficient unto themselves, having their own time and history. However, much resistance to whites had a religious dimension, although through changed religious sensibilities. Such transformations emphasize the dynamic nature of American histories throughout the human occupation of the continent, dynamics which are still unfolding today.

Australia

Another continent criss-crossed by religious connections, seen to be the tracks of ancestral spirits, is Australia. Australian Aboriginal people shared continent-wide forms of belief known to Europeans as the Dreaming (or to Aboriginal people as *Djukurrpa*). During the creation of the world ancestral spirits travelled, shaping the features of each region, including the physical aspects of the landscape, such as rock formations, rivers, stands of trees, or water holes, the plants and animals (many of the ancestors were sharks, dingos, or snakes, which then became the totem or sacred animal of the group concerned), and people.

Stories of the Dreaming concern not just the physical creation of the landscape, but outline correct forms of behaviour towards other species, landscape formations, and people. Dreaming tracks run right across Australia, linking people at great removes, and the tracks can be summoned up in song, painting, and dance (Bruce Chatwin's book *Songlines* provides a European evocation of this ritual landscape). What might appear to Europeans as purely pragmatic activity, such as hunting or gathering, requires respect for and connection to the spiritual powers of the land. The Dreaming connects people to a timeless, but ever-present, past. Archaeological evidence indicates long connections, with some rock art motifs probably 30,000 years old still in use today. Stone tools, the major source of evidence from Australia, were imbued with aesthetic and spiritual qualities through colour, brilliance, and the potency of their source, challenging to the prehistorian more at home with understanding the flaking and cutting properties of stone than their cosmological significance.

The first European accounts of Australia were of park-like landscapes; open grasslands dotted with trees. For Aboriginal people grasslands were useful as they provided seeds, but also bulbs and tubers; their major sources of meat, such as kangaroos and wallabies, ate grass. Grassland was encouraged through burning. But the landscape was not purely or mainly pragmatic and in recent accounts people talk about cleaning the country through fire. Fire is an ally: ceremonies exist for it, with great knowledge lying behind its use.

Due to the rapid extirpation of Aboriginal people on contact with Whites, much of the Australian landscape was reverting to forest by the middle and later 19th century when it was cleared, giving Europeans a false sense of what the country had been like (an excellent account of Aboriginal land care practices is contained in Bill Gammage's *The Biggest Estate on Earth*). But there is now good evidence that fire was used by Aboriginal people throughout their 50,000 years of occupation of Australia, giving the lie to the idea that the Australian landscape today is a basically natural one, from which hunter-gatherer groups took what was offered to them. While not farming, Aboriginal land care was long term, systematic, and aimed towards a relationship with the country which was both physically and spiritually sustaining.

People put fire to use, but also water. In Victoria in the southeast of the continent over the last 6,600 years at least, Aboriginal people have been digging channels several kilometres long to alter water flow, and then building structures out of local lava to hold water in ponds and to create traps. Europeans first noted this early in their encounters with the Victorian landscape. George Augustus Robinson, who had the title Chief Protector of Aborigines, reported that on 9 July 1841, to the north of Gunditjmara country at a swamp near Mt William, he encountered:

> an immense piece of ground trenched and banked, resembling the work of civilized man but which on inspection I found to be the work of the Aboriginal natives, purposefully constructed for catching eels.

The ethnocentrism in this observation has also permeated 20th-century attempts to construct an archaeology of Australia.

It has taken some time for archaeologists to realize how far Aboriginal people shaped and altered the landscape. Large numbers of eels and other fish could have been harvested through these complicated traps, which either helped support relatively sedentary populations or occasional gatherings of clans for ceremonies (or some combination of these). Eel traps are being put forward for World Heritage status. In places like Victoria there is evidence of relatively fixed territories and possibly large, sedentary groups along the Murray River and its tributaries.

Much about the Australian landscape and its histories require recalibrated assumptions on the part of non-indigenous people. Australia's oceans are incredibly rich and varied, so that it is no surprise that some of the most striking features of archaeology are large shell middens, which were well investigated around Sydney, the Northern Territory, and Queensland. Early research on middens took a very functionalist stance, with interest in what species were collected, how far these can inform on changing conditions of coast and river systems as sea levels stabilized over the last 4,000 years or so, how much food the meat in the shells produced, and so on. These are all valid questions, but more recently, partly because archaeologists are working more closely with indigenous people or indigenous people are training as archaeologists, things like middens have been rethought.

Ian McNiven's recent work in the Torres Strait has helped reinterpret shell mounds. This is a 150-kilometre-wide stretch of sea and islands that separates Australia from New Guinea, comprising a rich tropical region with a maze of coral reefs abounding in fish, shellfish, turtles, and dugongs (a marine mammal weighing around 400 kilograms). Many different mounds are found, some mainly composed of dugong bones, others of shell and fish bone, and others still contain a broader set of debris. McNiven points out that many relations compose the mounds: those between humans and non-human species, which have a totemic or cosmologically charged aspect; relations between men and women when gathering, cooking, and consuming food; important moments in the life of the individual as they are initiated into the group, or the history of the group.

Mounds are not composed of rubbish in our terms, of material that can be disposed of and not thought about, but of culturally charged items that need to be treated with care as bearers of important histories and relations. As people pursue everyday tasks in the villages on islands like Mabuyag in the Torres Strait, the middens are a constant reminder of past important events and indicate those to come. In areas such as Weipa on the west coast of Cape York, mounds many metres high have been accumulated; monumental reminders of vital relations between humans, non-humans, and ancestors.

Australia has one of the great bodies of rock art in the world, with dramatic clusters not just across the tropical north and desert centre, but occurring across the continent. Rock art changes over time, but also shows continuity, with different styles emerging over many millennia. Rock art combines the geometrical and the figurative. It is difficult to date, but a combination of an analysis of the changing styles, super-position of images, and some absolute dates allow decent sequences to be developed. Early phases of art in Arnhem Land depict creatures long extinct; a subsequent 'Dynamic' phase shows humans carrying weapons, wearing clothing, and often leaping or running; later still humans have features of yams—all of these styles were probably painted before the end of the Pleistocene and it is only in later styles that ancient artists painted creatures like crocodiles and fresh water fish found today.

The earliest styles give us a window on Pleistocene life in Australia, although presented through the cosmological lens then current. Large, elaborate headdresses of the so-called Dynamic-style figures indicate forms of personal decoration and ceremony unknown from later periods, demonstrating how much of the complex histories of Aboriginal Australia we have lost.

Compared to the Americas, movement into Australia and New Guinea was early, taking place at least 50 kya. Australia and Papua New Guinea were joined at periods of lower sea level until 8 kya into the giant landmass known as Sahul, but have always been separated by sea from the island archipelago of present-day Indonesia. The biologist Wallace, a contemporary of Darwin's who came up with a theory of evolution, recognized the huge differences in plants and animals between southeast Asia and Australia.

The Wallace Line divides the placental mammals (monkeys, elephants, tigers, etc.) of southeast Asia from the marsupials of Sahul. The history of continental drift created the super-continent of Wallacea (composed of Antarctica, South America, southern Africa, India, and Sahul) on which marsupials developed and then broke it up, so that Antarctica drifted south and froze, killing all animal life, and all the other continental fragments bumped into other continents (North America, northern Africa, and Asia) which had large, carnivorous animals which promptly ate all the marsupials. Australia reached its present position some ten million years ago and remained isolated enough by the northern seas to deter the entry of placental mammals.

Humans were the first species to cross this major biogeographical barrier, entering a world of plants (the gums, acacias, etc.) and animals completely new to them. There was a great range of environments across Sahul which stretched from the Equator to sub-Antarctic regions of southern Tasmania, including the Highlands of New Guinea, the highest mountains east of the Himalayas, and the massive central deserts. Sahul represents a laboratory for testing out modern human capabilities, tests which our ancestors passed with ease, so that by 40 kya there were groups hunting up by glaciers in central Tasmania, in the temperate zones of southeastern and southwestern Australia, well into the desert, and all over the tropical north. Not long afterwards they reached islands off present-day Papua New Guinea, where I have spent some time digging caves. These have revealed some of the earliest marine fishing in the world, and evidence of island occupation maybe at a similar time to the first island colonization of the Mediterranean, and rather earlier than the Caribbean.

Papua New Guinea and the Pacific

The last major portion of the world to be settled was not a continent, but the Pacific Ocean. Movement of people into the Pacific created new ways of being in the world with their own sets of physical skills and sensitivities to the physical and human worlds. Europeans can sail and navigate at sea through technological inventions and innovations, the concrete outcomes of problem-solving intelligence. Charting latitude is a tale for Europeans of timepieces, astronomical observations, and charts. Very different skills were developed by Pacific peoples. How was it that the biggest of all oceans, the Pacific, was crossed, starting some 3.5 kya and completed with the settlement of Hawai'i, Easter Island, and New Zealand, less than a millennium ago? The necessary skills and abilities have a long prehistory.

In 1985, I was digging a site called Matenkupkum, a spacious, dry cave on the east coast of a place called New Ireland, one of the larger offshore islands of Papua New Guinea. The cave is metres from where the Pacific Ocean crashes onto the reef, and while digging I could look out of the cave aware that, directly ahead of me were thousands of kilometres of open sea. The next landfalls are the tiny islands of Kiribati (formerly the Gilbert and Ellice Islands), easy enough to miss, and then no land until the western seaboard of North America. Matenkupkum's name translates as the 'cave of the swifts' due to the birds that nest in fissures in the roof of the cave, one point on their long-distance travels across the globe.

In the upper archaeological levels of the cave, large coral limestone slabs had been laid as the foundation for a hearth, much as people do today. Local people digging with me speculated excitedly as to which ancestor was responsible for this hearth and why they had no stories concerning such a thing. Connected with the hearth were large numbers of bones of wallaby, cuscus (a tree-dwelling marsupial), rats of a nicely edible size, thousands of shells from the reef, together with the bones of reef and deep-sea fish, and numbers of rather crude stone tools, including small flakes of obsidian.

Much of the deposit we dug out was ash from the hearth. Here was evidence of a camp, where people hunted animals on the grasslands and rainforest behind the cave, but mainly gathered shellfish and fish from the reef below. The obsidian came from the volcanoes of adjacent New Britain some 350 kilometres away: an indication of longer-distance connections in a mass of material obviously local. About a metre below the layers of the hearth was a deposit of a different type. Local stone tools were still there, as were fish and shellfish, but the only land animals were the bones of snakes and lizards and there was no obsidian. Material was much less abundant, without any evidence of hearths or burning.

These lowest levels we later dated to 35 kya. People must have sailed into New Ireland, which was always an island even at periods of lowest sea level, making this one of the oldest pieces of evidence of island colonization in the world. Similarly, the fish bones and shells were evidence of some of the oldest marine fishing and shellfish gathering in the world. Not that age was everything, but here were unusually precocious maritime traditions, which provided a long backdrop to the large-scale, but recent, open-ocean colonization. The uniqueness of the Pacific island evidence was soon reinforced when we learnt that the northern tip of the Solomon Islands had been occupied almost 30 kya, which involved a journey over the horizon, overcoming a considerable psychological barrier.

Skills of voyaging and navigation are only part of what was needed for successful island colonization. Islands generally have fewer plants and animals than larger landmasses, and foodstuffs can be scarce, so that getting to islands can be difficult, but staying alive once there can be even harder. The earliest inhabitants of Matenkupkum lived from a small number of lizards, snakes, and birds as the only terrestrial foods. People overcame these constraints by moving themselves between scarce resources, living a mobile lifestyle in which the sea was vital as a source of food and of movement. After 21 kya, things changed and we started to find the bones of the grey cuscus, an arboreal marsupial, and evidence of obsidian from neighbouring New Britain. We know that the obsidian was imported, as no sources exist on New Ireland, but it seems too that the grey cuscus was also an import, soon to be joined by a new wallaby species, both ultimately originating from mainland New Guinea.

Such imports represent a new strategy. Instead of moving people between resources, resources were now moved to people. These were groups thought to be hunter-gatherers, yet they were certainly not passively suffering the constraints of their environment, but actively overcoming it, through moving around wild animals (and possibly plants) together with important materials such as obsidian. Pacific prehistorians talk of transported landscapes in relation to the smaller islands of the remote Pacific, all settled in the last 3,500 years.

When sailing to Tonga, Tahiti, or Easter Island, colonists loaded their canoes with root crops like taro and yams, trees such as breadfruit and bananas, and the pig, dog, and chicken. The first few centuries after landfall saw considerable replacement of the natural plants, the extinction of indigenous birds (the moa of New Zealand being the best known case), and their replacement with introduced plants and animals, often planted and used in ways that mimicked the original flora and fauna, giving some protection to these fragile ecosystems. What Europeans took to be natural paradises in places like Tahiti or Samoa were some of the most carefully managed landscapes on earth.

The origins of these transported landscapes can be traced back to the evidence from Matenkupkum some 21 kya, as can the evidence for seafaring and fishing which goes back 35,000 years. The ability to move freely by sea and to cope with relatively restricted sets of resources on islands laid the basis for island life not found anywhere else in the world, showing that there were quite separate traditions of life developed in various parts of the globe.

A major extension of human settlement in the Pacific occurred with the so-called Lapita phenomenon. From around 3.5 kya people settled in places like New Britain and New Ireland, often living in stilt villages out over the reef and creating pottery with extremely complex geometrical decorations, but also shellfish hooks and a range of ornaments. Such villages are found from the offshore islands of New Guinea to Tonga and Samoa, where they are the first indications of human habitation. As is often the case, we are uncertain about the status of Lapita villages. They were inhabited for a millennium or more by people who combined plants and animals from the land with food from the sea. The striking decoration of the pots and other forms of material culture are very similar (indeed identical) over some 3,500 kilometres. We might be dealing with a super-community, through which obsidian and other things were exchanged, possibly with shared beliefs.

The later settlement of the Pacific, which has proceeded over the last 2,000 years, set up a known network of seaways, which people traversed regularly, despite the extraordinary distances involved. Perhaps the most famous instances of Pacific early histories are the Easter Island (Rapanui) statues, which, together with the temple platforms on which they were placed, are variants of sacred complexes known from across the central Pacific and have nothing to do with South America, despite what Thor Heyerdahl argued so passionately.

We have now reached the end of the long process by which humans colonized the world (it is notable, but coincidental, that places like Iceland were settled around a millennium ago, at much the same time as Hawai'i and New Zealand (Aotearoa)). Settlement was never a passive process of accepting what was found in a place, but of active engagement with new possibilities and constraints. People need to stay alive, but the logics within which they worked included an understanding of, and debate about, the nature of cause and effect in the world, which was often cast in cosmological terms. Debate and inventiveness, which includes a great range of symbiotic relationships, are central to human success in both moving and creating sustainable lifestyles in novel places, some continental landmasses, others tiny islands.

Chapter 7
Final thoughts

Rethinking our deep past is underway. An older scheme emphasized progress, but has been challenged both from empirical evidence and new thoughts on what it means to be human. Prehistory, viewed through the lens of progress, saw humans as attempting to exert control over the world and increasing their ability to do so. Farming was a great leap forward, in allowing for food production, rather than taking from the environment what was on offer. Increased craft production, the creation of cities, and eventually industrial mass-production all saw increments in human abilities to extract, shape, and use matter and energy.

A necessary or inevitable corollary of changing productive arrangements was an increase in human hierarchy to chiefdoms and then the emergence of class through the state. Humans started mobile and gradually settled, differentiating their material worlds and social relations in the process. A further important idea in these older schemes, often implicit rather than directly stated, was that humans in all times and places worked with a form of practical logic. The need to provide shelter, food, and order were so great in early history that people were mainly concerned with how the world worked in terms of means-ends relations. Religion or cosmology were secondary attempts to understand some of the broader mysteries of life.

Many of us would now reject the notion of progress and the assumption of increasing rational human control that lies behind it. Rather, people are seen as part of the world, enmeshed in a great network of relations needed to sustain life, but which unfold through working as much with other entities as against them. Human engagements take many different forms and create varied ideological entailments. It is only in the last few centuries in places like Europe that pragmatic logics have dominated and are taken for granted.

For much of deep human history people have developed a feel for the physics, chemistry, and biology of the world (as we would label them), but saw kinship between themselves and other things, living and non-living. Staying alive involved an interchange and partnership between people and the world, not a purely extractive mentality. Human life was not always in harmony with the rest of the world or with other humans. There are clearly deep contradictions in the needs of varied people and significant others that result in violence and death.

Given the complexity and unpredictability of human relations there can be no overall direction to deep history, so that people move between wild and domesticated foods, settle for a while in large aggregations which they then abandon, try out technologies in some periods that later may not suit them. We now live in vast large populations, many of us in cities, producing and consuming unsustainable amounts of things. This has come about relatively recently, through the last five centuries of colonialism and capitalism. Our lives are by no means an inevitable outcome of long-term human history. The present flies in the face of long-term trends rather than deriving from them.

The older progressive scheme gave us a sense of direction to history. We have now lost something of that, but can replace it with greater appreciation of human variety. Categories such as hunter-gatherers and farmers have become very constraining. Rather than asking in any situation whether the groups we are dealing with hunted or farmed, we should look instead at the full range of engagements people had with the people, plants, animals, and things around them, as well as how these engagements unfolded over time. Most of the long-term histories of most continents are best approached in this way, so we do not need to think about the hunter-gatherer status of the people who constructed Poverty Point in the Mississippi valley or of the Aboriginal people constructing eel traps in Victoria.

A first house-clearing move to make is to throw out subsistence-based categories—hunter-gatherer, farmer, pastoralist. It is hard and often impossible to categorize people in these terms, as we can now see. The productive base was thought to have political economic connotations. Hunter-gatherers formed egalitarian bands, farmers developed into hierarchical tribes and chiefdoms, which, with the emergence of cities and a more intensive agricultural and craft economy, became states. The subsistence categories are dubious and their broad entailments unpredictable from the point of view of the older model. People who we might classify as hunter-gatherers can form towns, but with no evidence of class divisions or clear social hierarchy. The so-called Three Age system of Stone, Bronze, and Iron Ages had its uses as an initial means of classifying a confusing richness of new evidence for those in the 19th and 20th centuries. Even in Europe, where it worked best, divisions of time masked continuities between periods. All people who use bronze do not do so in the same manner, so that we do not really know what we mean by a Bronze Age. There was also a colonial politics to the older scheme, which wanted to rank people from primitive to civilized. Although such a desire to rank human groups has broadly vanished, the older categories have lived on. Now is the time to jettison them and start again.

Our new start will involve fewer presumptions about human history. We are interested in the breadth of various human engagements, with plants, animals, materials, and other people.

These engagements are unpredictable and impossible to control. We find here common cause in a new biology, one that is moving away from any form of genetic determinism towards notions of gene flows between species and a process-based view of ecology. We also do not know what a human body can do, either on its own or in resonance with other bodies. We are replacing an idea that intelligence is in the head, with a stress on the skills of the body activated by the properties of different materials. Skilled bodies appreciate the world through action and making. As an inseparable part of this process the world acts back on us and an appreciation of the world often takes a holistic form, which we talk about in terms of aesthetics and beauty.

Materials and bodies can be thought of in terms of their forms, but we are also looking at flows between generations—of the genetic materials of living things or the elemental composition of things like metal as it is either recycled or deposited. Notions of flow incite us to think time is a crucial dimension of all action, and that change unfolds through varying rhythms.

Areas for new research and thought

Both empirical and theoretical issues emerge from our rethinking of deep history and I shall look briefly at some here.

We have evolved as a set of multiple species. Since we split from our common ancestors with the apes, there have been multiple sets of hominin species and it was only with the extinction of the Neanderthals that *Homo sapiens sapiens* are alone. We do not know what relations we had with our cousins and we cannot assume that they were always antagonistic or competitive. Relations may not have involved deliberate working together, but some symbiosis is likely through landscape alteration, the movement of materials, and influences on the distributions of plants and animals. Earliest human history all took place within Africa. What we do not know for sure, from *Homo erectus* onwards, is the relationship between developments inside Africa and those outside.

It is possible *erectus* evolved outside of Africa, from earlier excursions of hominins we have not yet detected and then moved back in. The range of habitats *Homo erectus* is found in, from savannah to tropical rainforest, indicates a generalist at home in the world. The links between *erectus* and hand axes also show the manual skill and appreciation of form these creatures possessed and the movements of materials suitable for hand axes indicate a capacity for forethought. The possibility that some hand axes were made but not used, and that others were accumulated in large caches, indicates the power of performative action and the lure of skill, but also the aesthetics of the objects produced. We cannot think in contemporary terms, but there are aspects of making and deposition that go way beyond the purely functional.

We no longer see deep history as punctuated by a series of revolutions, starting with the Upper Palaeolithic where change was thought dramatic due to the development of fully modern humans. Instead, we see slowly evolving capabilities over the 800,000 years from the start of the middle Palaeolithic through to the Holocene. For the early part of this sequence an emphasis on continuity cuts any clear links between biological evolution and that of material culture, communication, and so on.

Hand axes were made both by *Homo erectus* and successor species as far as we can tell. Fully syntactical language may not have come into being until fairly recently, possibly with *Homo sapiens sapiens*, but complicated communication was possible much earlier. Youngsters may have learned to make hand axes through close observation, including some linguistic prompts or guides. The development of joint attention and intention are really crucial foundations of complex sociability. Making and using artefacts, together with the broader values they materialize, were important shared activities holding the group together;

shared activities allowed for the recognition of strangers whose practices differed.

Rather than great leaps forward we are looking at the slow accumulation of skills and capabilities, as much by the group as a whole as on the part of individuals. The development of skilled group action through the interplay between bodies and materials is the real stuff of human intelligence. Hominins set up a series of symbioses with the world which involve mutual recognition and understanding. Such symbioses eventually become, in some parts of the world, what we call farming, but only after experiments over vast stretches of time. Hominins have cycled through innumerable climatic changes, between warm and cold in the higher latitudes, wet and dry nearer the Equator. Constant adjustment and reworking of relationships have become basic to what it means to be human. Moving now into a newly warm period, caused by human action, we have considerable skills of adjustment. These are much harder to use than previously as there are now many more people in the world, with higher material expectations.

Much later, in the Holocene, there are a knot of problems around issues of sedentism and mobility, which might also involve power structures and hierarchy. There is increasing evidence from ancient genetics and isotopic analysis of human bone indicating the movement of people in the past. The evidence is complex and unfortunately interpretations are often too simple, suggesting migrations of whole human groups.

Late Neolithic groups, such as Yamnaya found in the steppe and Russia, which are poorly defined as an archaeological entity, are thought to have migrated west towards Europe, perhaps causing Corded Ware groups to also move in a domino effect. This evokes images of more recent migrations, such as wagon trains of white settlers across the plains of the US. Leaving aside the dubious associations of such a parallel in any case, there is no evidence that the group we called Yamnaya thought of itself as a group or ever engaged in joint and coordinated action, like a migration.

We are left with a problem: on the one hand, evidence of human movement is increasing; on the other, the means we have of interpreting such movements are clearly flawed. A number of new ways of thinking about human movement come from our reconsideration of the evidence. One of the features we can now observe, from at least the late glacial Natufian period onwards, is that people aggregate into sedentary sites. Aggregation happens both among those groups dependent on wild foods and those with some or many domesticates.

Aggregation is followed generations or centuries later by dispersal and once we get to sites of the size of the Cucuteni-Trypillia sites in Moldavia and the Ukraine (see Chapter 5), where several thousand people lived. Both the clustering together and subsequent dispersal would have had significant demographic effects in periods when the population was low overall. Such pulses of population aggregation would have moved people across the landscape, causing new modes of arrangement and connection in the process. Humans and their genes would have moved.

These forms of aggregation are hard to explain, but my feeling is that they were connected to power. Our notions of aggregation and power have become skewed by our own contemporary and recent historical experience. Today we live in a world of cities. About half of the world's population inhabits cities, which produce three-quarters of the global gross national product, but also about 80 per cent of global greenhouse gas emissions. It is not surprising that we might want to read past forms of aggregated living through a trajectory that ends up with the contemporary city.

This is a mistake: many of the arrangements of the past were radically different from anything today. In 1950, Gordon Childe wrote one of the most cited pieces ever written by an archaeologist—'The Urban Revolution' in the journal *Town Planning Review*. Here he laid out a checklist of ten points that distinguished cities from other settlements, which included their size, the existence of full-time specialists supported by the surplus of a group tilling the soil, monumental buildings, long-distance trade, writing, and the existence of a ruling elite. The elite linked cities to another major concept, that of the state. Cities were organized by class, not kinship, with the labour of the majority exploited by the minority to create rich material culture and impressive buildings to which most had no access.

The creation of cities and states, first in Mesopotamia and then Egypt, but soon in other areas such as the Indus Valley and China, were the crucial steps, it was assumed, in making the world of the past look more like that we know today. There was a continuity between these earliest cities and those of the contemporary world, it was argued. Childe's thoughts have been incredibly influential and still structure our discussions of the city today. But this is too proscriptive a checklist of features, creating a binary distinction between city and not-city. Apart from anything else, there is an ongoing and not especially productive discussion about whether a large settlement is a city or not—is Neolithic Çatalhöyük with probably 1,000 inhabitants 9 kya, but no writing, monumental buildings, etc., a city? Both positive and negative answers have been given.

These discussions are unproductive and I think we need to broaden our considerations to look at the aggregation of people, plants, animals, and materials over the last 10,000 years attempting to understand their causes and consequences in a manner that allows us to probe their circumstances, not seeing them as steps on the road to modernity.

Discussions of the city have been tied up with the origin of the state, the emergence of class society, and hence differences in power relations between groups. Many large agglomerations display little or no evidence of ranking within the group. House sizes are much the same across all the examples we have looked at, from Natufian settlements through to PPNB mega-sites, Çatalhöyük on the Konya Plain of Turkey, the Cucuteni-Trypillia sites, and Poverty Point in the Mississippi valley. What these sites might indicate is ranking *between* groups. Some groups were able to control the movements of materials, but especially to gain a command of ritual that picks them out from their neighbours.

Mega-sites involve an intense ritual life, as we saw from diverse examples from Göbekli Tepe to Cahokia. Some, such as Cahokia, seem to have had a colonial aspect, setting up sites with the same ritual preoccupations around water and astronomical alignments in the far north of the Mississippi valley. Tapping into basic powers of the universe is a powerful means of drawing people to you, who will disperse once belief in such an experiment wanes, as it always does. The millennial aspects of mega-sites seem key to their creation and decline, both of which are often rapid.

A further feature of many earlier Holocene societies is the levels of violence within them. The massacre site at the Neolithic site of Talheim, Germany, is unusual but not unique, and is complemented by widespread evidence of injuries to the skeleton, some of which were fatal and some debilitating. Rick Schulting has estimated that levels of violence in Neolithic Europe may have exceeded that of most known ethnographic groups, indicating again that relations between groups were volatile and dangerous. Indeed, the indications of widespread exchanges of fine stone and other materials from the Palaeolithic onwards are evidence of the efforts put into alliance building and peacemaking, which were necessary because the basic state of society was one of war. Earlier human life exaggerated both the positive and negative aspects of sociability: both the best of times and worst of times are to be found among people from the late Palaeolithic onwards.

Movements of people cannot be thought about separately from the movements of living things and materials. There are great areas of interchange in the world—the steppe, the Indian Ocean, Mesoamerica, and the Mediterranean, to name but some. Interchange happens because the conditions of connectivity are there, but also because there are engines of innovation in places like Africa, southeast Asia, and the steppe itself, generating new relations with plants, animals, and materials. Plants and animals could be moved in a wild state and sometimes domesticated outside the areas of their wild occurrence. Seafaring, and possibly sailing, is a Palaeolithic development, opening up the Mediterranean and its islands, allowing the colonization of Australia at least 50 kya and movements into and around Pacific islands for the first time around 35 kya. Perhaps surprisingly, land travel faced greater barriers, so that the domestication of the horse some 6 kya opened up the steppe to people, a fact reinforced by wheeled transport a little later; the camel allowed desert travel by people and their goods, something that became increasingly important as deserts dried up after the middle Holocene. That despised animal, the donkey, has been a vital carrier of loads across Eurasia and Africa for many millennia, being domesticated perhaps twice in Africa maybe 6 kya. The history of agriculture and of trade would be quite different without the hardiness of the donkey, able to cope with rough terrain and lack of water.

Not only have plants and animals moved, but so too have materials, the earliest evidence being of stone over short distances many millions of years ago. By the Holocene, stone moved long distances from many sources and we can see that metals, such as bronze, flowed over Eurasia from at least 5 kya. The movement, use, and reuse of materials is important, so that we can visualize streams of bronze crossing Eurasia, crystallizing into axes, sickles, or daggers along the way, but then often being melted down and used again.

We need to think both big and small, with long-distance movements of materials, then made into artefacts in a great range of local variants. A technology like bronze smelting and casting involved also charcoal, wax, and clay at the least, so that the rolling mass movement of bronze had effects out into the landscape, influencing the care and control of forests, bee keeping, and taking clay from river valleys. Once again a change in one area rippled out across the landscape, interacting with alterations in other areas of life. In Africa, and possibly the Americas, people's relationship with metals differed and may have been more localized and episodic, prior to the last few thousand years when larger-scale cities and states come into being.

Since the last glaciation we can see two trends in tension with each other. On the one hand are all the movements of species and materials that I have just outlined, so that no one area can be understood in isolation. Human lives are fundamentally shaped by the mobility of all sorts of things and the novelties these movements generate. Counter to this is the creation of many local ways of life, with their own values, valences, and characters. Movement might have led to a homogenization of human cultural forms, with similar things, skills, and practices found everywhere, but it did not. On each continent people have grown intimate with local plants and animals. The llama, the sweet potato, and the chilli formed the nutritional basis and the zest for people's lives in South America in a manner analogous to, but nevertheless different from, the cow, millet, and beer in Africa.

The continents saw different explorations of human capacities through local involvements with the world. This is only partly because the material resources of each continent varied, but also due to the logic of magic, myth, and transformation in each region. Every continent has gone off in its own directions, with Australia and the Americas taking quite different paths to Eurasia and Africa, which were connected by the movement of people, plants, animals, and things. Divergence has not precluded the movement of people, ideas, and things, but has meant that acceptance of outside novelty depends on how things resonate locally.

Much rethinking is needed concerning power, aggregation, and the movements of people, plants, animals, and materials. Each cannot be thought about separately—great streams of people migrating across the steppe, prairie, or savannah are unlikely and unusual. The pulsations of aggregation and dispersal acted as a pump in many areas; the negotiations of peace and alliance between groups moved materials and people; the possibilities offered by a new animal species, such as cattle in Africa, or a novel material, such as bronze across Eurasia, set up varied networks and relations which shifted movements again.

A constant problem people faced was that of order. Given the plethora of relations in which we all live, and the fluxing nature of those relationships, how do we impose some order on the world? One means of stabilizing the world was through the imposition of form. One of the most famous and longest-lasting instances of form was also one of the earliest—the hand axe. A defined form, such as a stone tool flaked from both sides, with a point at one end and a rounded, heavier counter-balancing end which fitted into a hominin hand, needed a very particular choice of raw materials, and a defined sequence of actions to make, which then influenced how hominins were able to use it. A hand axe both enabled action and constrained it. The more skilled the user, the greater the range of possibilities inherent in the form. Many hand axes look beautiful to us, an obviously ethnocentric statement, but the symmetries of the form may have appealed to earlier ancestors too. The accumulations of hand axes, some unused, indicate that the performance of making may have been appreciated, although quite what appreciation of skill meant half a million years ago is a thought-provoking question.

Technologies are reinvented in new situations into which they were introduced. A prime example is the introduction of bronze working into China from the steppe. China was somewhat late in accepting bronze, but engaged in extremely sophisticated production of pottery, such as the eggshell-thin black wares of the late Neolithic Longshan group along the Yellow River. There also existed a well-defined set of ceramic ritual vessels for presenting and drinking various liquids. These ceramic forms were remade in bronze, keeping the same basic shapes, but with much greater elaboration of form and decoration. Jessica Rawson has pointed out that the size and weight of bronze vessels would have required very particular bodily interactions in the processes of ritual, so that performance was created by the objects as much as the people in charge of the ritual. The Chinese Bronze Age was unlike any other, making us wonder whether the term 'Bronze Age' is usefully comparative.

Domestication might be also seen as a stabilization of form, encouraging also a greater predictability of behaviour. The history of domestication, especially of animals, but to a lesser degree of plants, is being rethought. In an important article, Larson and Fuller review animal domestication, showing it often occurred accidentally, as animals are drawn into new, more intense relations with people as human lives change.

The animal most obviously domesticated by mobile peoples is the dog, which derived from grey wolf populations, presumably drawn to people by food, but both human and wolf must have developed practices that were mutually advantageous some time in the late glacial. Some animals were preyed upon and the close relationship and understanding of the other established by hunting allowed for commensalism. This may be true of llamas, alpacas, turkeys, and Muscovy ducks in various parts of the Americas, so that, for instance, ducks may have been attracted to humanly created ponds and canals in southern South America before becoming domesticated around 4 kya.

Recent genetics is also showing that genetic alteration was often first seen in variability of the colour of the feathers, coat, ears, and face, hinting that there might always have been an aesthetic dimension to our relationship with these animals. Domestication may not have been due to deliberate human design, but was appreciated and continued for the predictability it brought to relations between humans, animals, and plants.

Insect domestication is a small but important area, with the first artificial hives occurring in Jordan about 3 kya, but probably indicating a much older relationship, perhaps when bees were attracted to gardens and fields. The Chinese silk worm is now totally dependent on human feeding and rearing, a relationship that had started at least 6 kya.

A further element of order occurs through what we call art. In a number of cases, from the complex decorations on Lapita pottery some 3.5 kya in the western Pacific, to the so-called Scythian and Celtic art styles across Eurasia in the first millennium BC, to the striking use of form and colour in the US southwest associated with the Great House phenomenon in Paquimé and related sites, we can see complex sets of motifs, linked to defined forms of metal, pottery, or stone with special uses connected to ritual. Just as Chinese ritual bronzes enjoined defined forms of action in a sequence, so too did other fine metalwork or pottery.

Objects we call art did not exist in a vacuum, but were used and deposited on sites with their own structures and histories, which gave spatial and temporal shape to human lives. There is much to interest us in the history of aggregation and settling down, but there is a complementary history of movement, which is a complex phenomenon in huge, relatively homogenous spaces, such as the grassland steppe or Pacific Ocean.

It is clear that for the nomadic pastoralists of Asia movement was not random, but had seasonal and longer rhythms we are only starting to understand. Sites such as kurgans or the Mongolian khirigsuur were important markers of the landscape, formed of complexes of mounds and surrounding stones in circular or rectangular patterns. These are sometimes in association with so-called deer stones (human forms decorated with deer) found in Mongolia and the Altai region of Siberia.

The khirigsuur complexes sometimes have cardinal orientations and may be connected with human burial. They have complicated histories, with groups returning to them through the second millennium BC, so that they formed spatial focuses of action but also punctuations in the life of the group, such as that occasioned by the death of a prominent person. In a totally different cultural context, the mounds of northern Australia and the Torres Strait help shape the history of the groups that made them, with emotionally heightened ritual practices an important sedimentation of history into the bodies of the group.

Forms of artefacts, of plants, animals, and places, all help create a geography of linked places and a temporal shape to past, present, and future. Such shaping is always in tension with the more accidental and unexpected conjunctions of the world: events intrude into the most structured of societies. Our intelligence derives from a sense of the orderliness we try and impose and the experimental quality of action always confronting the world as it changes.

We act as if we are separate from the world, when in fact we live within it and it within us. A story of the deep past that emphasizes increased human control over the world is not just empirically untenable, it also reinforces our belief that attempts to control the world are a natural part of being human. People in the past did not live in harmony with each other or the broader landscapes in which their lives unfolded. There were too many contingent factors and contradictions for life to be harmonious. However, as well as conflict they sought kinship with the things around them and any extractive attitude was often balanced by notions of moral responsibility to other entities. The deep past has no easy lessons for the present, except that life often had an experimental aspect, constantly playing with relations with significant others. The study of our past can and should challenge our common-sense assumptions by which we live in the present, opening up the possibilities of new and different ways of living in the future.

Further reading

Chapter 1: Rethinking prehistory

P. R. Smith and S. Mrozowski (eds), *The Death of Prehistory* (Oxford University Press, 2014): a series of essays discussing the colonial heritage of the notion of prehistory and the deleterious effects of the idea as far as indigenous peoples are concerned.

Chapter 2: The history of prehistory

V. G. Childe, *What Happened in History* (Penguin, 1942): classic account of human history by the most influential archaeologist of the earlier 20th century.

L. Malafouris, *How Things Shaped the Mind: A Theory of Material Engagement* (MIT Press, 2013): an original analysis of notions of human intelligence, stressing the links between the human body and material things in generating our understanding of the world.

G. Stocking, *Victorian Anthropology* (Free Press, 1987): dense, but excellent account of the debates of the 19th century and their social context.

B. Trigger, *A History of Archaeological Thought* (Cambridge University Press, 2006): the most comprehensive account there is.

Chapter 3: In the beginning—African origins and global movements

R. Dennell, *The Palaeolithic Settlement of Asia* (Cambridge University Press, 2008): a scholarly but comprehensive account not just of the Asian evidence, but also its African antecedents.

C. Gamble, *The Palaeolithic Societies of Europe* (Cambridge University Press, 1999): an intelligent and detailed account of the earliest prehistory of Europe.

C. Gamble, J. Gowlett, and R. Dunbar, *Thinking Big: How the Evolution of Social Life Shaped the Human Mind* (Thames and Hudson, 2014): a clear and detailed account of a large-scale investigation into the Palaeolithic evidence for evolution and its implications for human intelligence.

M. Pitts and M. Roberts, *Fairweather Eden* (Century, 1997): an excellent account of the work, personalities, and findings at Boxgrove.

C. Stringer, *The Origin of Our Species* (Penguin, 2012): clear account of human evolution by an accepted expert in the field.

Chapter 4: The long-term history of Europe and Asia

G. Barker, *The Agriculture Revolution in Prehistory: Why did Foragers Become Farmers?* (Oxford University Press, 2006): the only global review of farming systems; takes a more nuanced view of hunter-gatherers and farmers than the title implies.

B. Finlayson and G. M. Warren, *Changing Natures, First Farmers and the Modern World* (Duckworth, 2010): both a critique of the idea of hunter-gatherers and an account of the late Palaeolithic and early Holocene in the Middle East.

D. Fuller and M. Rowlands, 'Ingestion and Food Technologies: Maintaining Differences Over the Long-Term in West, South and East Asia', in J. Bennet, S. Sherratt, and T. C. Wilkinson (eds), *Interweaving Worlds—Systematic Interactions in Eurasia, 7th to 1st Millennia BC. Essays from a Conference in Memory of Professor Andrew Sherratt* (Oxbow Books Ltd, 2011), pp. 37–60.

C. Gamble, *Origins and Revolutions: Human Identity in Earliest Prehistory* (Cambridge University Press, 2007): a sustained critique of the idea of revolutions in the Palaeolithic and early Holocene.

L. Liu and X. Chen, *The Archaeology of China: From the Late Palaeolithic to the Early Bronze Age* (Cambridge University Press, 2012): the best and most up-to-date account in English of China's prehistory.

S. Mithen, *The Prehistory of the Mind* (Thames & Hudson, 1996): emphasizes the importance of mind rather than bodily intelligence, but provides a lively and interesting account of this important subject.

A. Moore, G. Hillman, and A. Legge, *Village on the Euphrates* (Oxford University Press, 2000): the site report on Abu Hureyra—large but worth the effort.

Chapter 5: Continental fusion—connections across Europe, Asia, and Africa

D. Anthony, *The Horse, the Wheel and Language: How Bronze Age Riders from the Eurasian Steppe Shaped the Modern World* (Princeton University Press, 2007): detailed but accessible account of the archaeological and linguistic evidence of Eurasian prehistory.

C. Broodbank, *The Making of the Middle Sea: A History of the Mediterranean from the Beginning to the Emergence of the Classical World* (Thames and Hudson, 2013): a superb account of the history of the Mediterranean down to 500 BC.

B. Cunliffe, *By Steppe, Desert and Ocean: The Birth of Eurasia* (Oxford University Press, 2015): beautifully written and illustrated account of the connections forming Eurasian societies.

P. Mitchell and P. Lane, *The Oxford Handbook of African Archaeology* (Oxford University Press, 2013): a comprehensive set of essays on Africa's prehistory and early history.

C. Renfrew, *Archaeology and Language* (Jonathan Cape, 1987): this book rekindled archaeologists' interests in the history of languages and put forward the hypothesis that the spread of the major language families was due to the movements of farmers.

Chapter 6: New worlds—the Americas, Australia, and the Pacific

P. Hiscock, *Archaeology of Ancient Australia* (Routledge, 2008): a recent and full account of the archaeology of the continent.

P. Kirch, *On the Road of the Winds* (University of California Press, 2002): a comprehensive and accessible account of Pacific prehistory.

D. Nichols, *The Oxford Handbook of Mesoamerican Archaeology* (Oxford University Press, 2012): an excellent set of accounts of the prehistory and early history of central America.

B. Pascoe, *Dark Emu, Black Seeds: Agriculture or Accident* (Magabala Books, 2015): an Aboriginal author challenges the labelling of Aboriginal people as hunter-gatherers.

T. Pauketat, *The Oxford Handbook of North American Archaeology* (Oxford University Press, 2012): a collection of essays with are both factually sound and engage with the debates around the material.

T. Pauketat, *The Archaeology of the Cosmos: Rethinking Agency and Religion in Ancient America* (Routledge, 2013): gives an excellent account of Cahokia and related sites, as well as arguing for the importance of religion to human culture.

Chapter 7: Final thoughts

G. Larson and D. Fuller, 'The Evolution of Animal Domestication', *Annual Review of Ecology, Evolution and Systematics* 45: 115–36 (2014): a provocative new take on animal domestication.

Index

Index